God Can
Heal
You Now

Also by Emily Gardiner Neal

A REPORTER FINDS GOD THROUGH SPIRITUAL HEALING

God Can Heal You Now

EMILY GARDINER NEAL

PRENTICE-HALL, INC.
Englewood Cliffs, N.J.

© 1958 by
Prentice-Hall, Inc., Englewood Cliffs, N.J.
All rights reserved, including the right
to reproduce this book, or any portions
thereof, in any form, except for the inclusion
of brief quotations in a review.
Library of Congress Catalog Card Number 58–12861
Printed in the United States of America

35748

First printing . . . . September, 1958
Second printing . . . . . . April, 1959

DEDICATION

To my husband Alvin Willard Neal
and
for the Glory of God

Acknowledgments

SPECIAL thanks go to my husband, Alvin, and our daughter, Diana, whose patience, understanding and interest did much to facilitate my work; and to Ethel T. Banks, for her unfailing help, encouragement, and faith.

I take this opportunity to acknowledge my incalculable and continuing debt to the Rt. Rev. Austin Pardue, D.D., Bishop of the Diocese of Pittsburgh; and the Rt. Rev. Wilburn C. Campbell, D.D., Bishop of West Virginia. The ministries of these great Churchmen have served as never-failing beacons, leading me, as they have led many others, from the rocky shoals of cynicism and disbelief into the safe and quiet harbor of the Holy Spirit.

To all those too numerous to mention individually, who have given me so freely of their time and cooperation in the preparation of this book, I am deeply grateful. Without their assistance it could never have been written; and without their witness, it would never have been written.

—EMILY GARDINER NEAL

Contents

PART II

Healing Ministries

PART I

Spiritual Healing

CHAPTER 1

Twentieth Century Miracles

CMIRACULOUS healings reminiscent of the New Testament are occurring in churches of every denomination all over the United States. They are the result of a revival of one of the Church's oldest and most dynamic ministries— the healing of sick bodies as well as sick souls. This ministry of the early Church, though never wholly lost, has been mislaid for many centuries. It is being rediscovered today with thrilling results.

A woman suffering from brain cancer, diagnosed by an internationally known clinic, was given about one year to live. She attended a healing service in a Methodist church and claims she was healed. She has suffered no symptoms over a period of six years.

A victim of advanced tuberculosis, medically diagnosed by

every known laboratory method, and bedridden for sixteen months, received Holy Unction from an Episcopal minister and was back at work in five days. His health has continued good for the seven subsequent years.

A child, paralyzed from the waist down as a result of polio, was carried into a Baptist healing service and walked unaided out of the church. This was four years ago, and he still has full use of his limbs.

A man with a heart hopelessly crippled from rheumatic fever received the laying-on-of-hands from his Presbyterian pastor, and fully recovered.

Overcoming skepticism

The immediate reaction of outsiders when confronted with alleged religious healings of this kind is complete incredulity. This was exactly my reaction when the phenomenon of spiritual healing came to my attention several years ago. In the first place, I had considerable scientific background, having worked extensively with private doctors and in hospital laboratories. In addition, as a magazine feature writer, I had specialized in scientific reporting. "Miracles," which imply the breaking of natural and scientific laws, obviously didn't make sense. Furthermore, I was an agnostic, and the claim that healings of supposedly incurable disease were the result of the direct intervention of the Holy Spirit seemed to me fantastically childish nonsense at best.

However, as the stories of healing continued to mount, my curiosity was aroused. Always on the lookout for a provocative article idea, it occurred to me that an exposé of the dangers and fraudulence of faith healing might make a good magazine piece. I therefore decided to do a little investigating. What began as a brief and cursory examination of the subject eventuated in several years of the most intensive research I have ever done.

I interviewed hundreds of people, including medical doctors, physicists, clergymen and laymen; I examined scores of case histories. As time went on, the cumulative evidence of genuine healing gathered. I procured medical substantiation (in the form of X-rays, lab and hospital reports, state compensation records and doctors' statements) for dozens of healings of organic and congenital diseases, including cancer, tuberculosis, and congenital bone deformities. Finally I had to admit that there seemed too many of such healings to ascribe to coincidence. Nor could the cured diseases be glibly written off as instances of wrong diagnosis, or casually dismissed as imaginary or psychosomatic.

Midway in my research my contemplated "exposé" was mentally drafted into a "report" on the phenomenon of non-medical healing. But while I could no longer deny that some sort of healing force was in operation, I continued for a long time to deny emphatically its connection with God.

In seeking the source of these religious cures, however, I ultimately found myself forced into a study of Christianity. Gradually, to my own considerable surprise, it began to make sense. I continued into a study of the early post-apostolic Church, which led me into an understanding of the theology which lies behind the healing ministry. I finally came to accept its validity.

The outcome of this exhaustive study and investigation resulted not in a skeptic's exposé, nor in an agnostic's report on a phenomenon—but in a book which is the story of an unbeliever's journey into faith: *A Reporter Finds God Through Spiritual Healing.*

What finally convinced me that these healings were of God, were the result of the direct intervention of the Holy Spirit? It was my gradual realization that when the body was so cured, there was an undeniable healing of the spirit. In lives profoundly changed after a spiritual healing, I recognized the Holy Spirit at work. In the deep spiritual regenerations I witnessed, I acknowledged the Hand of God.

Spiritual healing not new

There is nothing new about faith healing. It has been practiced in one form or another for thousands of years. Many were the sick treated, and probably helped, at the temples of Aesculapius, legendary Greek god of medicine. Many have been the sick treated and possibly cured by witchcraft. Many are the sick today, who by faith in an amulet, a well-phrased slogan, or their doctor, are physically improved.

But there is a vast difference between these kinds of "faith" healings, and today's revived healing ministry within the Church. Spiritual healing does not concern itself with the curing of the body alone with no reference to the spirit; nor yet is it the type of metaphysical healing which affirms the spiritual at the expense of the physical. Spiritual healing deals with the cure of the *whole* person—body, mind, and spirit. Its goal and purpose is the seeking of a closer relationship with God—the soul's salvation. When the *spirit* is healed through faith in and through the power of the Risen Christ, healing of the mind and body follows as an expected corollary.

The tremendously thrilling thing which is happening today in churches all over the world is not from any new concepts or revolutionary ideas. It is a reaffirmation of an indisputable Christian truth: that the salvation Our Lord came to bring us is *total* salvation. It includes the curing of the body as surely as it does the healing of the spirit and the saving of our souls from sin.

The prophets had foretold that healing would be a mark of the New Age—the Day of the Lord—and it was. Jesus confirmed the prophecy of Isaiah: "He will come and save you. Then the eyes of the blind shall be opened, and the ears of the deaf shall be unstopped" (*Isaiah 35:4–5*).

Why should we have so long overlooked Our Lord's emphasis on healing as an integral part of our redemption? Why so long ignored the fact that nearly two-thirds of the Gospel is devoted to His healing work? Again and again we are told that none who came to Him remained unhealed, and that "as many as touched Him were made whole." Of profound significance is the fact that He did not intend that the healing of the sick, any more than the preaching of the Kingdom, should be confined to His earthly Ministry and should end with His life among men. As He charged His followers to preach the Gospel to all creatures, so did He charge them to heal the sick wherever they went (*Luke 9:2–6*). The indivisibility of healing and the Kingdom is made crystal clear as time after time we see that "He received them, and spake unto them of the Kingdom of God, and healed them that had need of healing" (*Luke 9:11*).

The story of the healing ministry of the Church begins in the Book of Acts, which records the prodigious healing work of St. Paul and St. Peter, to whom the multitudes flocked, "and they were healed every one" (*Acts 5:16*).

The history of the healing Church is continued in the writings of the early Christians known as the Fathers of the Church, who have given us eye-witness reports of the healing activity of the early post-apostolic Church, where for three hundred years after Christ physical healing was the rule and not the exception.

Then began controversy, growing disunity, diminishing faith. Gradually, healing within the Church ceased. She was forced to rationalize her failure to heal by claiming that the healing gift of the Holy Spirit had been withdrawn. It was then that the Church began unwittingly to "minimize His Holy Name."

New recognition of spiritual healing

Today's renascence of the healing ministry, then, marks the return to a fundamental part of Our Lord's teaching. It is a reacknowledgment of the nature and will of God as unmistakably revealed by His Son, the revelation disregarded for so many centuries.

Individual clergy all over the world have for two thousand years offered isolated instances of His healing power. The great Catholic Shrines have kept alive the knowledge that He heals today as surely as He did during His earthly ministry. But it is only recently that a rebirth of spiritual healing, as a part of the Church's official ministry, has taken place. This renascence is church-wide. There is probably no branch of the Christian Church which has not at least some churches practicing the healing ministry, and the number is increasing every day.

The present revival is still in its infancy, but it is already of such proportions as to have engaged the attention of many scientists. Healings of so-called incurable disease have led an increasing number of medical men to ask a cogent question: "Does a healing power actually exist?" More and more physicians of the caliber of Dr. Robert Laidlaw, chief psychiatrist of Roosevelt Hospital, New York City, find themselves in accord with him when he answers an unconditional "yes."

Dr. Loring T. Swaim, instructor at the Harvard Medical School for twenty years, comments that "A sick soul can thwart the best medical treatment." The American Medical Association recently put its stamp of approval on this point of view, by issuing to its membership a pamphlet dealing with the importance of religion in treating the sick. This leaflet discusses the vitally important role of religious faith in healing, and urges the close cooperation of clergy and doctors. It gives many examples of healings where faith in God, and prayer, were acknowledged by the attending physicians as decisive factors in the patient's recovery. With emphasis being placed on the desirability of "more fully correlating the body and spirit," medicine has officially recognized the importance of the spirit in the total health picture, and the role of God in healing.

As in medicine there is a growing belief that man is a trinity composed of body, mind, and spirit, so is there in all other branches of science an increasing tendency to accept, at least as a strong probability, the existence of spiritual forces operating in the world, even if as yet they can be neither weighed nor measured. A number of physicists agree with Dr. Henry Margenau, of the Sloane Physics Laboratory, Yale University, when he says: "I believe that the ultimate truth will not be found in physical science alone, but in the convergence of science and religion. The old view, that para-normal phenomena are intrinsically irreconcilable to the scientific viewpoint, is on its way out."

Dr. Margenau answers those who think, as I used to, that all religious belief is founded on blind faith, and all science is based on infallible reason and incontrovertible proof. "The most fundamental of scientific axioms," he observes, "are only postulates. Even the laws of arithmetic are not empirically true, but are based on hypotheses which today *seem* true, but tomorrow may be disproved. Accurately speaking, we must concede that a scientific commitment is based on faith as well as reason—just as religion is based on reason as well as faith."

Fifty years ago it was considered scientific heresy to maintain that man might be motivated by spiritual forces as well as mechanistic ones; that there might exist spiritual as well as natural laws. Today such a proposition is held eminently respectable. Research engineer Julius Weinberger, of the technical staff of RCA laboratories, makes a no-longer revolutionary observation: "The phenomenon of spiritual healing is an example of the operation of spiritual laws which are superior to, but do not conflict with, scientific or natural laws. In my opinion. research relating to the human soul or spirit is the most important job yet to be done by science."

The fact that spiritual healing is gaining the approbation of an increasing number of scientists may seem immaterial or even irrelevant to the believer. My reason for emphasizing the scientific viewpoint is the fact that I was able to verify medically scores of alleged healings of supposedly incurable disease. This convinced me of the validity of the healing phenomenon and flung wide my heart to Christ. I believe that *my* story is the potential story of countless unbelievers. To the faithful, believing is seeing. For me, and I know for many, seeing is believing. I have personally discovered that while faith is indeed the *heart's* cognition, it is the *mind's* knowledge which often plants the seed.

To the believer, God is responsible for *all* healing, whether or not He is acknowledged. As a famous French surgeon stated, "I bind the wounds, God heals them." The healing Church emphasizes that His healing power is not confined to any one method, but is dispersed through various channels, which include medicine and psychology as well as religion. The working together of clergy and doctors is vitally important in order that all the tools He has placed in our hands may be utilized. But when medicine has failed and God has taken over, we see those dramatic healings which to an increasing number of people are unmistakable evidence of the direct intervention of the Holy Spirit.

Tangible evidence of God's healing power

Like most writers, it is my custom to "walk away" from an assignment once it is completed, and get on with the next job at hand. This I have been unable to do with the subject of spiritual healing. One does not casually "walk away" from the tangible evidence of the power of God, from the exciting revelation that He lives.

If my research for *A Reporter Finds God* was arduous and painstaking, it is no less so today, although for different reasons. In the first instance, I was investigating to *disprove* a premise. I now investigate to *prove*. Those who believe need no such proof. Many unbelievers, regardless of evidence, will continue to disbelieve. However, I think that much harm is done the cause of spiritual healing by careless and fallacious claims of divine cure. So that fodder shall not be provided for the skeptics; so that the operation of the Holy Spirit shall not be prostituted into chicanery; so that the healing Church may be protected from all danger of hysteria and any hint of fanaticism, I am convinced that every effort should be made to confirm medically as many healings as possible.

Honest objectivity, to be sure, is as difficult to find in science as in any other field. The scientist who is unalterably convinced that all the answers can be found in physical science and refuses to consider any evidence to the contrary, has a closed mind. He is as guilty of irrational fanaticism as the religious who disdains all scientific progress. Nevertheless, the true scientist who is not blinded by materialism; who strives to make the theories fit the facts, can be a strong ally of the healing ministry. He may appear recalcitrant in acknowledging the power of God, but by his very slowness to capitulate; by his rational objectivity, he may help to safeguard spiritual healing from unthinking emotionalism, from a dangerous lunatic fringe, which could degenerate the great healing ministry of Christ into a fanatical cult.

A year or so ago, I attended a dinner, and found myself sitting next to the managing editor of a large city newspaper. We talked of many things, none of them to do with religion, for I knew he was an atheist. Suddenly, during a lull in the conversation, I heard a woman across the table mention a healing she had recently experienced. Immediately the subject turned to spiritual healing. Learning of my interest in it, the editor turned to me with a look of complete bewilderment. Because he had always thought of me as a down-to-earth reporter who had done considerable editorial work for his paper, he asked several searching questions. This marked the beginning of a conversation which extended far into the night. Neither of us made the meeting which the dinner had preceded.

At the end of the evening the newspaper man asked if he could examine my files. "If what you say is true," he said as we parted on the hotel steps, "this is the most convincing presentation of Christianity I have ever heard."

54₀₀

Within the next two months, after attending many healing services, this man was to say, "My whole life has changed. I have found now what I have probably unconsciously sought all my life—evidence of a living Christ."

And so it was with me. Six years ago, cynical and unbelieving, I scoffed at "miracles." My cynicism was to fall before the truths of the Christian faith, made intelligible to me by the healing ministry. My unbelief was to shatter before the irrefutable evidence of the power of the living God.

During the past two years, in traveling extensively over the nation, I have seen many wonderful healings. The phenomenon is no longer new to me, but my sense of excitement and awe has not diminished. This book is the story of what I have seen, of what I have learned, and of what I believe to be true regarding the healing power of God.

Today, more clearly than ever before, I see in the healing Church the unchallengeable answer to the agnostic belief that Christianity is mere legend, born of man's need; or only a philosophy, a way of life; or solely an historical event which occurred and was finished two thousand years ago, to be interpreted or misinterpreted ever since. To know the healing Christ is to see Christianity transformed into what it is meant to be: a dynamic, living and demonstrable reality.

CHAPTER 2

God's Will for Us

OUR VERY FIRST step toward healing is to realize that God does not will our sickness. As the Author of good, not evil, He does not cause disease, nor does He inflict it upon His children as a means of punishment.

The unreserved acknowledgment of this tremendously vital truth serves as a stepping stone to spiritual healing. In my case, and I believe in many other cases, it has also led to an acceptance of Christianity itself. My agnosticism was due in no small measure to the fact that I simply could not reconcile a God whom I was told to love and trust with the suffering I saw about me. I used to marvel then, as I still do, at the fortitude of those who, with complete resignation and apparently without rancor, could say, "This is God's will," as they watched a baby die of leukemia, or saw a child crippled with polio, or a young wife ravaged by cancer.

To me it seemed impossible, and it still does, to love or serve or even acknowledge, a Creator who is the perpetrator of disease, with which He cruelly and indiscriminately harasses mankind.

It was my study of the phenomenon of spiritual healing which was to lead me to the truth which is setting thousands of Christians free from the heresy which has so long shackled Christ's power in His Church and in our lives.

Healing the body leads the mind to God

It was in my first serious study of the Gospels that I was to discover that Christ has revealed to us, beyond the possibility of any misunderstanding, the true nature of God: a God of infinite mercy and boundless compassion, a Maker who so loved the world that He gave His only Son to suffer and die, so that we who crucified Him might be saved (*John 3:16*); a creator who knows and cares when even one of His countless sparrows falls to the ground (*Matthew 10:29*); a Parent to whom each one of us is as beloved, no matter what our deficiencies, as though no other child exists in the world.

Jesus said, "Be ye therefore merciful as your Father is merciful." These were not idle words, for His entire ministry is a demonstration of their truth. Again and again He reminds us that He and the Father are one: "He that hath seen me hath seen the Father" (*John 14:9*). Wherever He went, He healed the sick, in mercy and compassion. Working ceaselessly to fulfil the will of God, Christ banished disease in His Father's Name, wherever He found it. He "went about all the cities and villages . . . healing every sickness and disease among the people" (*Matthew 9:35*). It is unthinkable that as the multitudes followed Him and He healed them all, that He was working against His own will.

Jesus came to bring God to us—to save our souls. As the Son of Man, He also knew the importance of our bodies. He then, as now, often began His saving work with a physical healing which would result in spiritual change. Time after time then, as it does today, the *visible* sign of the living God, turned those healed to their Lord.

Two thousand years ago a blind beggar received his sight and "followed Him, glorifying God" (*Luke 18:35–43*).

A palsied man took up his bed "and departed to his own house, glorifying God" (*Luke 5:18–26*).

The multitude "saw the dumb to speak, the maimed to be whole, the lame to walk, and the blind to see: and they glorified the God of Israel" (*Matthew 15:30–31*).

And so it is today. A steel worker, long deaf, receives his hearing. He now leads weekly prayer meetings at the mill. A business man, instantly healed of lung cancer, now devotes his spare time to witnessing for Christ. A hopelessly crippled attorney walks again. He uses his oratory now to teach a truth he has personally experienced: that Christianity is not a method for enduring illness; it is the means by which disease can be triumphantly overcome.

Our Lord makes it abundantly clear that disease is part of the structure of evil He has come to vanquish. He invariably speaks of sickness as something to rebuke, something evil and therefore contrary to the will of His Father.

"And Jesus rebuked the devil; and he departed out of him: and the child was cured from that very hour" (*Matthew 17:18*).

"He cast out the spirits with His word, and healed all that were sick" (*Matthew 8:16*).

To Jesus and His disciples, and to all the saints, Satan was a very real adversary. You may not believe in an actual devil, but you may concede that there seem to be a good and an evil force at large in the world, the latter continually opposing and hindering God's perfect will for us. This theory of Christian dualism, of God versus Satan, which has always been part of the faith, is one of the easiest of all Christian assumptions to accept. It does much to explain disease and suffering. It also helps to explain how, if God does not *will* disease, He appears to permit it.

God made the world, and He "saw that it was good." He also gave men free will. By the misuse of this great gift, evil came into God's creation, thus precipitating the battle between good and evil which has raged ever since. We are assured through Christ, however, that God *is* almighty and will achieve the ultimate and complete victory over sin, sickness, and death, which is assured us in the Resurrection. When this occurs, we will know in its full sense, the Kingdom of which He speaks. Meanwhile, we are catching a glimpse of it now through spiritual healing, as we witness with increasing frequency the conquest of the Holy Spirit over the evil that is disease.

Jesus commissioned the Church to heal

Our Lord leaves us in no more doubt of His Father's will concerning disease, than concerning sin. They are the two-headed enemy He labors unremittingly to overcome. The Gospels tell the story of His victory over both, a victory as unequivocal as His triumph over death itself.

But He never confined the conquest of sin and disease to His earthly ministry. He commissioned His Church to continue His work under the guidance of the Holy Spirit. He commanded His disciples to heal the sick with the same assiduousness with which they preached the Kingdom.

"He called his twelve disciples together, and gave them power and authority over all devils, and to cure diseases. And he sent them to preach the kingdom of God, and to heal the sick. . . . And they departed and went through the towns, preaching the Gospel, and healing everywhere" (*Luke 9:1, 2, 6*). Our Lord has left no room for doubt: the Kingdom of God and the realm of sin and disease cannot co-exist.

In traveling over the country and talking to hundreds of

people about spiritual healing, I have encountered considerable confusion over the phrase "Thy will be done."

It is curious that over the ages these potentially comforting
words should have developed a prevalent connotation that is
far from comforting to many people. "Thy will be done" has
long been prayed as a lugubrious accompaniment to hopeless
situations, and the phrase seems to have become a natural
corollary to disaster. We are so in the habit of using these
words out of context that we have overlooked their real significance, which is fully explained in the Lord's Prayer: "Thy
kingdom come, thy will be done *on earth* as it is *in heaven.*"

And what is His will in heaven? That "there shall be no
more death, neither sorrow, nor crying, neither shall there
be any more pain" (*Revelation 21:4*).

For centuries Christians have been taught that the words
"if it be thy will" are a virtually essential termination of all
prayer. They have become an inevitable part of our prayer
pattern. But while they certainly have their place, it is *not,*
according to the teachings of Christ, in *healing* prayer. There
are some areas in which we are not certain of His will, and
must seek through prayer to learn it; but this is not true of
sin and disease. Do we repent of our sins, concluding our
prayer with "if it be thy will"? Of course not. We *know* He
wills our repentance. Likewise, on the authority of His Son,
we are as certain that He wills our wholeness as we are that
He does *not* will that we go out and commit a murder. We are
as sure that He wills our body's health as that He wills our
soul's salvation.

To pray "if it be thy will" is to limit the power of your
healing prayer, for these are tentative, qualifying words, ex-
pressing doubt. They are the outward expression of an inward
lack of faith in God's desire and ability to heal us. Such a
prayer seems to indicate a lack of acceptance on our part of
Christ's revelation of God in respect to disease; for Our Lord
makes it clear that He healed always with the complete au-

thority of one who *knew* the will of the Father. He spoke the word of power, unweakened by a qualifying phrase.

"Arise and walk," He said. "I say unto thee, arise." Without hesitation, with complete conviction, He commands, "Receive thy sight;" and "Be whole of thy plague."

So should we pray, not in submissive resignation, but in certain confidence: "I know that thy will for me is perfect health. Therefore I receive my healing in the Name of Christ, so that thy will may be fulfilled."

Resist disease; do not accept it

Most of us are probably all too familiar with the necessity of resisting temptation, and the results if we do not; but the idea of resisting disease as also evil, comes as a new idea to many of us. It's not always easy, in either case, and it requires considerably more faith and effort than sitting passively by and saying, "thy will be done." But if you believe that disease, like sin, is evil, you will find yourself compelled to combat the one as fiercely as the other so that His will may indeed be done. The result is often a miracle of healing, such as I saw not long ago in a southern town.

The parents of a six-months-old baby, hearing that I was in the vicinity, asked me to go with them to the hospital to pray for their desperately sick infant. This was not an unusual request. A great many people ask me to pray for their sick, feeling that my strong faith in God's healing power will be beneficial. Many ask also that I lay on hands, but this I have thus far refused to do, because I do not believe that I am a channel for healing. In acceding to the request of these distraught parents, I explained this and suggested that we ask a minister to accompany us to perform this sacramental act.

Their reply was: "Oh no, there's no use in that. We know that Sandy's case is hopeless, and that it is God's will that he die. We just want your prayers for his soul."

I was completely taken aback. There was no time for me

to deliver a discourse on spiritual healing, as I was taking a plane out of the city within the hour; and I have never had the temerity to tell anyone how he should believe or must pray. It was obvious that the young man and woman were deriving a certain comfort, however small, from their resignation to the baby's fate. Dare I take it upon myself to interfere? Before I had actually made up my mind, I heard my own voice saying, "Look, there's every reason to think your baby is going to get well."

They both started. A sudden light flooded their eyes, then quickly receded. The father, belligerent in his despair, said, "How do *you* know? Do you know more than the doctors?"

"I only know," I said, "that it is not God's will that a six-months-old infant die. Will you just try to believe with me that He not only *wants* him to get well, but He has the power to *make* him well? We'll naturally pray for his soul, but let's pray for his body, too."

The young couple nodded, their eyes filled with tears.

We walked into the baby's room, and the three of us knelt by the head of Sandy's crib. I prayed a brief prayer, ending with, "In the Name of Jesus Christ, Sandy, you are healed." The infant stirred, and I had the complete conviction that he would recover.

Before leaving the hospital, I begged the young couple to stop saying to themselves, "He's going to leave us, but Thy will be done"—and, instead, to offer prayers of faith and thanksgiving that His will *was* being done, and the child was recovering. Without comprehension, but with a new hope, they agreed. I found out later that to everyone's surprise but mine, the baby made a good recovery.

Coincidence? Perhaps, if this were one, isolated case. But I have seen many cases where as soon as an affirmative prayer replaced the prayer of hopeless resignation, recovery ensued. We must acknowledge a causative connection between the expression of our faith in God to heal, which constitutes the prayer of power, and physical healing.

"*A thorn in the flesh*"

But, you may say, if it is so obviously God's will that we be healed, what about St. Paul's thorn? If God refused to heal His apostle, how can we possibly think that He will heal us?

An increasing number of theologians, spear-headed by the Reverend Frank Uttley, entirely reject the hypothesis that Paul's thorn in the flesh referred to a physical ailment: "and lest I should be exalted above measure . . . there was given to me a thorn in the flesh" (*II Corinthians 12:7*). They have reverted to the theory, held by a number of early Church historians including St. Augustine and St. Chrysostom, that the thorn was actually the sin of spiritual pride. These clergymen point out that the figure of speech "thorn in the flesh" is used only three times in the entire Bible. As in the first two instances it does not refer to physical illness, they ask, with undeniable logic, why its use in Paul's case should infer disease. They suggest, too, that the image of an invalid saint is not compatible with the Biblical picture of a titan missionary; a man apparently with the strength of ten, who endured shipwreck and persecution, imprisonment and stoning.

But the exact nature of the thorn seems relatively unimportant. What *is* important, is the fact that Paul was a man of overwhelming and unshakable conviction in the will and power of God to heal. His marvellous healing work, which included the raising of the dead, was as abundant as his preaching work, and was unequaled by any of the other apostles. In answer to prayer, God gave him strength for each day's needs—a strength with which any of us today would be well satisfied.

Whatever the thorn, whether disease or sin, Paul reaffirms the origin of both. He makes it perfectly clear that it was not placed in him by God, but sent by "the messenger of Satan to buffet me" (*II Corinthians 12:7*).

Occasionally I have wished that I could honestly believe that sickness is sent by God. Such a belief is an easy way out,

and it is not difficult to see how Christians have for so long
fallen into this line of least resistance.

In this connection, I remember a particular night several
years ago when the whole concept of spiritual healing was still
new to me. My husband was ill, and I had come home late
from the hospital after a long and discouraging conference
with his doctors. Completely exhausted, I threw myself on my
bed, thinking how relaxing it would be to accept passively
this illness as God's will, certain that there was nothing I nor
anyone else could do about it.

I felt far too tired even to pray, but lying flat on my back, I
leafed through the Gospels. When I had finished, I was more
convinced than I had ever been before that sickness, like sin,
is evil and must be fought to the finish, no matter how ex-
hausting the battle. It seemed to me I could not say that my
husband's sickness was God's will, without committing blas-
phemy; nor could I say "Thy will be done," and thereby wash
my hands of the entire matter, without violating what I had
come to believe was a fundamental Christian truth. I claimed,
that night, His wonderful promise: "Whatsoever ye shall ask
the Father in my name, He will give it you" (*John 16:23*).
He honored my faith.

Suffering is not saintliness

As I have been unable to discover any Scriptural evidence
whatsoever that God sends disease as chastisement, so have I
failed to find any indication that He sends suffering as a
means of spiritual regeneration. Indeed the Gospel evidence
seems completely to the contrary. Is it rational to suppose
that Jesus would have healed all who came to Him at the
expense of their souls?

We should never forget the Cross in Christianity, but
neither should its shadow obscure for us the joy of the Resurrection. While it is true that suffering is considered a part of
the Christian vocation, it is also true that we must differentiate

between redemptive suffering and purposeless pain. If we don't, we risk glorifying pain instead of the Risen Christ. But we don't have to make this difficult decision for ourselves. Jesus has already pointed the way.

Our Lord never said we didn't have to suffer. He healed the sick, but He warned us of persecution for His sake. He fed the hungry, but He said we who would come after Him must deny ourselves. He relieved the suffering, but He told us to take up our cross and follow Him.

He warned us of the pitfalls and temptations on the highway to His Kingdom, of the necessity for spiritual strength and moral stamina to complete the journey. Still He seems to make it clear that the battle against sin is an adequate testing ground for the soul, and the struggle toward holiness a sufficient crucible for the ennobling of the spirit.

As Christians we have tended to regard all pain, *per se,* as redemptive. For hundreds of years we have confused saintliness with suffering until the two have become synonymous in our minds; but, as the Reverend Dr. Leslie Weatherhead, prominent British Methodist, points out, it was not the suffering of the saints but their attitude toward it which determined their saintliness. Although their pain was not sent by God, they were able with His help to convert it to a holy purpose, offering their heroic endurance to His glory.

There are saints today. There is a woman in my city, declared by her doctors to be medically incurable. She has sought and received a magnificent healing of the spirit, but so far the healing of her body has not taken place. She is a tiny woman with a frail body, but she is a spiritual giant. All who come in contact with her feel humbled, strengthened and inspired. Having done all she can spiritually as well as medically, she has committed herself to God. She awaits His next step, not in submissive resignation, but in expectant faith and certain confidence that His love will ultimately free her from affliction. Meanwhile His grace is sufficient for her. She lives each day to His glory, offering to Him her patience, her serenity and her indomitable courage. His strength is made perfect in her weakness (*II Corinthians 12:9*). She transcends pain.

There are others like this woman whose suffering has tremendous redemptive power; but there are many more like the good churchman of my acquaintance who is ill from a duodenal ulcer.

For years he has felt a bitter hostility toward one of his office co-workers. His entire life, at home as well as at work, is colored by this continued resentment. Until his attitude changes, his ulcer will not heal; in fact, his doctor has implied as much. Yet this man piously declares that his illness is God's will, sent to strengthen him spiritually. Meanwhile, peevish and irritable, sick in both body and spirit, he makes everyone who comes within his range miserable by his complaining.

Now this type of suffering can no more be construed as redemptive than the stomach ache which follows the eating of too many green apples. There may be a certain *remedial* value in it, a warning to correct our faults—"for whom the Lord loveth he chasteneth" (*Hebrews 12:6*)—but there would seem to be little *redemptive* power in pain when it occurs as a direct result of our own unexpiated sins.

Redemption comes only when we tend our spirits as assiduously as our bodies; only when we are ready to correct, to change, to do His will.

The Reverend Edward Winckley, Associate Warden of the Order of St. Luke in South Africa, speaks from the vastness of his personal experience in the healing field abroad when he comments: "Unfortunately I have seen more illness used by the devil to further his own ends, than used for the glory of God."

Jesus suffered for us

There are those who argue that because Jesus suffered on the Cross, we, too, should suffer. In a sense this is true. Any sacrifice we make, whether it entails spiritual, mental, or physical pain, if suffered for Christ's sake, has redemptive power. But pain alone, simply because it is pain, does not, *ipso facto,* sanctify the sufferer.

Jesus never suffered for *suffering's* sake. He suffered to save us profitless pain. He "Himself took our infirmities, and bare our sicknesses" (*Matthew 8:17*).

He died for a cause, to free us from sin: He "who his own self bare our sins in his own body . . . that we, being dead to sins, should live unto righteousness" (*I Peter 2:24*).

As Anglican Father Winckley points out, Christian suffering is consequent upon trying to be a Christian; not suffering consequent upon disease. Therefore we must never confuse the issue by claiming that God sends disease for our spiritual benefit. This belief has caused thousands to suffer needlessly and die prematurely. As long as we think illness comes from God, we won't rebuke it; and as long as we think God has a purpose in our sickness, we won't resist it. As the Lambeth Conference on spiritual healing, held in England, reported: "In whatever way it [disease] may be overruled for good, it is, in itself, an evil."

Until the millennium there will be suffering which results from man's sin and ignorance, but this is a far cry from the idea of a loving God Himself sending disease.

The Reverend Richard Spread* makes the analogy of a human father who knows that his children will suffer. He certainly neither inflicts nor intends their suffering, but does all he can to teach them to avoid it. "You must fight against temptation," says the father, "no matter how hard the struggle, and no matter how much it hurts."

This human father does not first inject his son with cancer so that he may more effectively fight temptation. How, then, could we suppose that God could do so?—a God of whom Jesus says: "If ye then, being evil, know how to give good gifts unto your children, how much more shall your Father which is in

* *Stretching Forth Thine Hand to Heal.* London: Skeffington & Son, Ltd.

heaven give good things to them that ask him" (*Matthew 7:11*).

Jesus came in the Name of this Father, to bring us total salvation. To save means to make whole, both physically and spiritually. The body's healing and the soul's redemption were never intended to be separated. They are concomitant, as Christ has shown us, and as the Holy Spirit is demonstrating today through His healing power.

There is much of which we are not sure, but of this we can be certain on the authority of Jesus Christ: a maimed body is not a punishment, nor yet is it a prerequisite to the Kingdom of Heaven.

Disease is not the will of God, but the will of the enemy. It can be defeated at the Cross.

"I am the Lord that healeth thee." If you will believe that God wants you to be well, if you will pray the prayer of power, you will see that He has not changed.

CHAPTER 3

God's Healing Touch

$\mathcal{W}$HEREVER you are, whoever you may be, the healing power of God is available to you today just as it was two thousand years ago when "as many as touched the hem of his garment were made perfectly whole" (*Matthew 14:36*). On the basis of what I have seen, I am wholly convinced that there is no disease so "hopeless" that it will not respond to His almighty power, and no ailment so slight that it is unworthy of His healing love.

Once convinced that it is His will that we should be well, our next step is to release His healing power so that it may flow through us unimpeded. Successful spiritual healing depends primarily on love, faith, and repentance. These three factors are interdependent, but faith might be called the core of spiritual healing, as it is of all Christianity. It is only when we *believe* Jesus Christ was the Son of God that we can accept the reality of His resurrective power in our lives today. It is only when we *believe* what He told us of God that we can truly love our Creator. It is only when we *believe* what He told us of sin and its consequences that we can understand the necessity for repentance.

But no one knows better than I that this is easier said than done. The simple, child-like faith which Christ demanded of His followers, and upon which He tells us depends our entry into the Kingdom of Heaven, is incredibly difficult for many of us to acquire in this day and age. I know it was for me; but I think now that had I known in the beginning what I have since learned, the road might have been less rough.

True faith accepts the evidence

Not long ago someone said to me: "I only wish I had your blind faith. But I'll never have that complete faith necessary for healing."

This woman couched her comment diplomatically, but I knew exactly what she meant. I remember when I, too, used to envy people their "blind" faith. Yet at the same time I felt distinctly superior that my intellect prevented my being so gullible as they. I have learned since that faith need not and should not be "blind." It is not a superstitious credulity in an intellectually untenable premise. It begins, to be sure, where the mind ends and the heart takes over, but the distance between the two is not impassably vast.

While it is true that faith is trusting in some things which cannot be proved by scientific formula—the "substance of things hoped for, the evidence of things not seen" (*Hebrews 11:1*)—it is also, as Dr. Weatherhead emphasizes, "loyalty to the trend of all *available* evidence." My faith, then, is an acceptance of the evidence that God lives. This abundantly available evidence is to be found in the restored bodies and recreated spirits of those He has touched with His healing hand.

There are some who do not believe because they *will* not. But to those who do not believe because they *cannot,* Our Lord reveals Himself today as unmistakably as He did when He appeared before His doubting disciples, and said: "Behold my hands and my feet, that it is I myself" (*Luke 24:39*).

Through the revival of the healing ministry we have been immeasurably blessed. We are living in a scientific era, but not since the time of Christ have so many been so sure that He lives. We are living in an age of reason, but not since the early post-apostolic Church have the tenets of the Christian faith appeared so eminently reasonable to so many minds.

My friend was also mistaken in her assumption that *complete* faith is necessary for healing. I think that there is actually no such thing as "complete" faith. If it were complete it would no longer be faith, but certainty. As an essential part of the man-God relationship, it must be by faith and not through knowledge, that we reach Him. "Thy faith hath saved thee," (*Luke 7:50*) Christ said. He says it still.

Faith is many things. It is our confidence in the integrity of Jesus Christ when He said that He was the Son of God. It is accepting as valid His promise when he said: "Ask, and it shall be given you; seek, and ye shall find; knock, and it shall be opened unto you" (*Luke 11:9*). It is placing our reliance on His assurance of a healing God. It is putting our trust in a Person, certain that He is worthy of it.

I have found that nowhere is it more clearly illustrated than in spiritual healing, that God rewards those who "diligently seek Him" (*Hebrews 11:6*). Jesus honors the desire to believe, as well as the fulfilment; the striving to accept, not only the achievement; the seeking and not only the finding.

Complete faith unnecessary for healing

Fortunately for most of us, our healing does not depend on the *amount* of faith we have. Our Lord assures us that faith as small as a mustard seed can move mountains (*Matthew 17:20*). It can also create healing miracles.

A young married woman was scheduled for radical surgery on a Tuesday morning about two years ago. A biopsy had revealed a malignant tumor in her left breast. On the Friday preceding her operation, she attended a healing service at her church. "You could have fitted my faith on a pinhead" was the way she expressed it. "I went to church fairly regularly but I had never before gone to a healing service. I really went this time only at the insistence of a friend."

During the service she felt a sensation "like electricity" streak across her chest, then center for an instant in her left breast. When she arose from the altar rail, she reports: "never in my life have I had such a feeling of indescribable well-being and joy. I knew that something wonderful had happened to me inside. My friend said I had been healed, but just then it didn't seem to matter whether I had been physically cured or not."

That evening the young wife told her husband what had happened. "He just laughed," she said, "until he looked for the lump and found it gone."

The next morning the couple went together to the doctor who after careful examination declared that the growth seemed to have "mysteriously diminished in size." At his suggestion, however, she entered the hospital on schedule for another biopsy. The report came back negative.

This woman's faith and that of countless others like her may have seemed less than a mustard seed, but it was enough for God to work through.

I have witnessed again and again Our Lord's merciful response to mankind's age-old and despairing cry: "I believe; help Thou mine unbelief." It was a father bringing his sick child to Jesus for healing who first uttered those words. A compassionate God extended His healing hand then, and He is no less merciful today.

A year ago an anguished father, whose small son was suffering from an inoperable brain tumor turned to God, offering Him what he had of faith augmented by desire and hope. It was enough. Week after week prayers were offered for the child as he received the laying-on-of-hands. His condition steadily improved. A month ago the doctors who had said there was no hope pronounced him completely well.

"Thy faith hath made thee whole" was the keynote of Our Lord's earthly healing ministry. From what I have seen I believe that faith in some form is always necessary for healing today, although I am well aware that occasionally some are healed who appear to have no faith whatsoever.

Take the case of a man scheduled for surgery for a severe stomach ulcer, who frankly admits that he attended a healing service merely to please his wife.

"Oh, I believed in God as an idea—an abstraction," he says, "but I had absolutely no faith in a personal God. Furthermore, I thought all this talk of 'miraculous' healing was absolute bunk."

Nevertheless, to his own stupefaction, the intense pain of his ulcer subsided as he knelt at the altar rail. A subsequent X-ray revealed that he was healed. No surgery was required.

Now this man himself may have lacked faith, but his unbelief was routed by the massed faith of the believing worshipers who knelt beside him in the church. Here, of course, is the tremendous value of the church service. There is inestimable power in corporate faith. The almost palpable aura of expectant trust which characterizes a healing service not only increases the faith of the believers but seems to "rub off," as it were, on the unbelievers. If miracles are created through faith, faith, likewise, is created by miracles. Those healed do not remain unbelievers. They go on their way, like the blind beggar, "glorifying God."

I saw a man healed of a crippling arthritic condition. Supercilious, scornful, in full accord with the Communist dictum that all religion is the opiate of the people and spiritual healing the apotheosis of crackpot-ism, this man attended a healing service out of a hostile curiosity. Unsought, unbelieved, complete healing came to this man. Why? Simply because the faith of the people around him was stronger than his doubt? Not entirely. It is cases like these which have led me to believe that one of the great purposes of today's manifestation of God's healing power, is conversion. This man and others like him are now among the Church's most dedicated workers, converting hundreds of unbelievers by their witness for the living Christ.

But the conversions wrought through spiritual healing are not confined to self-confessed agnostics. Like the man with the ulcer, there are thousands who have conceived of God purely as principle—an empirical hypothesis. Through their awareness of His healing Presence, they have a new and exciting sense of the reality of Jesus.

There are thousands more who have believed the theological Christ, but have never until now known and loved Him as their personal Saviour. These have discovered the power which is Christianity. It is in this conversion from a mere philosophy to a dynamic, power-filled faith that we see most dramatically illustrated the primary purpose of spiritual healing: the bringing of souls to God.

Physical healings, important as they are to the afflicted, are only corollaries to the healings of the spirit. A cured body is not an end in itself. To regard it as such or to seek it as such is to do violence to the entire concept of spiritual healing. As Dr. Michael Ash, Harley Street surgeon, comments: "The healing of the body is only a temporary cure between life and death; the ultimate cure is always of the spirit."

Repentance opens the door to healing

Jesus admonishes us to "seek ye the kingdom of God; and all these things shall be added unto you" (*Luke 12:31*). This is why faith alone is not sufficient. Faith unlocks the door to His power, but it is repentance which opens it.

"Preach ye the kingdom and heal the sick," Our Lord commanded. "He that believeth is saved." He also added that "repentance and remission of sins should be preached in his name among all nations" (*Luke 24:47*); for "except ye repent, ye shall all likewise perish" (*Luke 13:3*).

"But surely you don't believe all that ridiculous stuff," said an old friend whom I hadn't seen for years. "What on earth has happened to your reason?"

Yes, I *do* believe it now, and *because* of my reason.

No one understands better than I, who was myself a skeptic so short a while ago, the prodigious difficulty of believing what Christ said simply because He said it. But the healing ministry is based on this premise. Because I, with my own eyes, have seen the incredible power in His words believed, the astounding results of His promises claimed, it seems to me now a clear-cut case of cause and effect; a question of "By their fruits shall ye know them."

If we accept the validity of Our Lord's mission, and practice in so far as we are able what He tells us, we find the fruits of the Faith. If we emasculate His teaching, selecting what we want to believe and rejecting what we would prefer to discard, we find ourselves left with a powerless ideology instead of a dynamic religion.

The subject of our own sin is one of those phases of Christianity which most of us would probably like to forget, if not actively reject. But the destructiveness of sin and the salvation of His forgiveness, are the substance of Christ's teaching, the heart of the Christian Church and an inextricable part of the healing ministry.

"Thy sins are forgiven thee," Jesus said to the palsied man. "Arise, and take up thy couch" (*Luke 5:20, 24*).

"Confess your faults one to another . . . that ye may be healed," said James (*James 5:16*). Throughout the history of the Church healing and repentance have gone hand in hand.

It is through repentance that we draw close to God. It is through His absolving power that our souls are healed. During His earthly ministry, Jesus never refused His healing grace to a sinner, nor does He now. It is never the sin, only our lack of penitence which blocks us from God and His power. To deny our sin is to deny our salvation, for we cannot be saved from what we don't have.

What sin is

"But what *is* sin?" a friend said to me in genuine bewilderment. "I haven't *done* anything."

In his mind my friend, like a great many of us, associated sin with a concrete, nefarious act, like robbing a bank or committing a murder. In the sense of committing a penitentiary offence, he certainly hadn't "done" anything; but he had broken God's law. Just how he had done so was divulged during the course of our conversation.

Sin is disobedience to God, of which, in one way or another, we are all guilty. It is impossible to live a sinless life, but our salvation lies in the attempt.

Even in seemingly inconsequential things, such as eating too much or drinking too much, or smoking too much, which overindulgences might appear to concern only ourselves, we are breaking His Commandment to "Love thy neighbor as *thyself*"; for we are harming our bodies—desecrating, if you will, the temple of the Holy Spirit.

But as Bishop Austin Pardue of Pittsburgh emphasizes; "Although the sins of the flesh should not be minimized, the sins most frequently overlooked are the sins of the spirit." Hostility, resentment, anger, fear, jealousy—these are the things which most flagrantly violate the law of love issued by Our Lord. To break this law, is to commit an offense against God, and to suffer the consequences of physical disease as well as spiritual sickness.

My friend, for example, told me that he had suffered for two years from a painful kidney ailment, which despite treatment from one of his city's most eminent urologists, had grown progressively worse. His condition at the time we met was threatening to incapacitate him, and, as he put it, "If I have to stop working my family will starve. I'm ready to try anything, even God." This is certainly not an ideal reason to seek God, but it is not an uncommon one. Innumerable people have been healed as they learn just what "trying" God involves.

During the course of our luncheon my friend also told me of a bitter professional disappointment he had suffered two years before. He spoke with rancor of the rival who, by using distinctly unethical methods, had procured the job for which my friend had long worked.

Turning to me, his face flushed with unforgotten anger, he said, "You can see why I feel the way I do, can't you?"

Of course I could, but however understandable his resentment, it was not justified in the sight of God. He had broken the law of love, and appeared to be suffering the consequences.

With some embarrassment, not relishing my role of arbiter of someone else's "sin," I pointed out this possibility. He looked at me for a moment without speaking. Then he said; "You know, that may make sense at that. Only last week my doctor told me that anger could seriously aggravate my condition. He questioned me, but at the time I never thought of this incident I just told you."

"Whosoever shall smite thee on thy right cheek, turn to him the other also" (*Matthew* 5:39) may be considered poor business practice, but it is good health insurance.

The force of humility

A man who was a firm believer in the power of God to heal suffered what appeared to be a minor injury to his shoulder. He received a number of heat treatments from his doctor, but the pain, now radiating into his left arm, grew constantly worse. He then tried an osteopath, with no success. Finally he consulted an orthopedist, who, after X-raying him, concluded that the pain was caused by pressure on a nerve in his neck. It was recommended that the patient be placed in traction. The patient agreed to be hospitalized immediately upon his return from an urgent business trip which could not be postponed.

By his third day away, the pain in his arm, no longer controllable by codeine, had become insupportable. He took the morning off to attend a healing service at a local church.

"As the minister prayed and laid on hands," he relates, "something came to me in a flash of enlightenment. I suddenly realized that I felt tremendously resentful toward a newcomer in my office who I felt was threatening my position. At almost the same instant, and I can't tell you *why* I did it, I found myself praying for this man and asking God to bless him. As I prayed, I felt a sensation of burning heat race down my arm. The pain seemed to seep out my fingertips, along with the heat. I haven't had a twinge since that moment. Incidentally, that man in the office and I have become close friends!"

The saints all put their finger on pride as the great spiritual culprit. As the most common of the sins which beset us, and the most dangerous because it is so insidious and far-reaching in its effects, it might not be too inaccurate to say that pride is actually behind and responsible for all sin. It leads to the exaltation of our own egos to the point where we worship ourselves and our achievements instead of the Creator of both. This tendency leads us into the greatest sin of all, a willful separation from God.

Pride has nothing to do with the self-respect which Our Lord surely meant us to have and to maintain, or He would never have issued His Second Commandment. Pride means the sort of self-aggrandizement which precludes humility. Humility is the very basis of our relationship with God.

Without humility we cannot have true faith, for faith presupposes complete confidence in someone other than ourselves. Without humility we cannot love God, for love is a humble desire to please the loved one. It is lack of humility which makes us deny our need of penance. It is lack of humility which makes it so difficult, not only to seek out our faults, but having discovered them, to confess them. Whatever other virtues we may possess, if we do not have humility, we are lost; whereas, however grave our faults, if we are humble enough to confess them, we can be saved.

A housewife, a veritable "pillar of the Church," suffered from seriously impaired vision from hardening of the arteries in the eyes. Her ophthalmologist declared that the damage done was irreversible, and his prognosis was eventual blindness. The patient, however, refused to accept this verdict as final. She knew too well the marvelous power of God to heal.

For some six months she sought spiritual healing through prayer and the sacramental healing rites of the Church, with no result, physical or spiritual.

"I couldn't understand it," she said. "I felt that there was a definite block in me which was hindering God's power, yet I couldn't put my finger on it. One day I sat down and really tried to think it through. *I* didn't smoke or drink like Mrs. S, who did both. *I* never missed a Sunday in Church, and Mrs. X missed at least once a month. *I* gave twice as much to the Church in time and money as did Mrs. T.

"Suddenly, as I went on in this vein to myself, I had the answer. It was my smugness; my self-righteousness; my intolerance; my *pride* which was the trouble.

"Next day I went to the healing service, and for the first time in many years of church-going, I had a real sense of the sin I was asking to have forgiven. I received the laying-on-of-hands with the first *honest* humility I think I had ever felt. Kneeling there at the altar rail, I felt His Presence as I never had before."

Slowly but surely this woman's vision improved. Today, four years later, it is normal.

"As many as received Him, to them gave He power," (*John*

1:12). And again and again it is being demonstrated that we
cannot receive Him if the door to our heart is closed by un-
repented sin. But in our desire to open it, so that His healing
power may be freed, we must guard against a neurotic over-
emphasis on our shortcomings as Christians. To remain perpetually on our knees in penitence, is to have misunderstood
the act of contrition, which is in two parts. For it is as important to be able to *accept* His forgiveness, as it is to *ask*. While
it is true that "If we say we have no sin, we deceive ourselves,"
it is no less true that "If we confess our sins, He is faithful
and just to forgive us our sins, and to cleanse us from all un-
righteousness" (*I John 1:8, 9*). It is not, therefore, in an un-
healthy state of continual self-condemnation that we will find
healing. It is in our joyful acceptance of His absolving grace.

Love fulfils the power of God

If faith evokes the power of God in our lives, and repentance releases it, it is love which ultimately fulfils it.

Wherever I have seen the healing ministry at work, I have
observed the limitless power of love in action. Through today's manifestation of the Holy Spirit, many of us worship
for the first time what we know to be the living God. We no
longer have to struggle to love a disembodied Spirit or an
Infinite Mind. We know Him now as He has been revealed
in the Gospels. We have felt the touch of His gentle Hand,
and we have known the comfort of His undeniable Presence.
Through our knowledge, then, of the living Christ, we have
learned to truly love the Father. As our love meets the love
of God, from which all love derives, miracles are wrought.

Time and again, in telling me of their healings, people have
said in surprise: "You know, I wasn't even thinking of myself.
I was praying for the person next to me, when I was healed."

The experience of a middle-aged woman who had suffered
a serious heart condition, is typical of His love, reflected however palely in our own actions.

"As I knelt at the altar," she said, "I could see that the woman next to me was in obvious pain. I was so anxious that she be healed that I forgot to pray for myself and prayed for her instead. While I was praying, I felt such peace and joy flood my entire being as surpasses description. I found myself almost running home and suddenly realized that I wasn't short of breath."

A few days later this woman had another X-ray and cardiogram made of her heart. She had been healed.

In mentioning healings of this sort to a clergyman with a great deal of healing experience, he commented: "Yes, that's why when I lay on hands or administer Unction, I like to have other loving members of the family present to pray with me. I have seen patients literally *loved* back to life."

You may find the healing Christ at home, through daily devotions; or at church, through the healing Sacraments; or through the intercessory prayer of others. But whatever the method, the road to Him will be the same—a highway opened by faith, cleared by repentance and illuminated by love. Thousands have traversed this road before you, daring to claim His magnificent promise: "Verily, verily, I say unto you, He that believeth on me, the works that I do shall he do also; and greater works than these shall he do" (*John 14:12*). He has honored their faith, and He will honor yours.

There is much we have to learn of the operation of the Holy Spirit, but these things we know: if we confess our sins, however inconsequential they may seem, to Him who has promised us forgiveness; if we try to meet His love with ours; if we offer our lamp of faith to Him, however dimly it may seem to burn, He will fill us with His healing grace. On this earth we may not see His Face, but as we step into the light of His healing Presence, we can know the end of darkness.

CHAPTER 4

The Healing Sacraments

God's healing power is not limited to any one church, nor is its channeling confined to any one method. However, today's healing Church has discovered the tremendous effectiveness of the Sacramental healing rites used in the early post-apostolic church: the laying-on-of-hands and Holy Unction.

Not long ago a member of a non-sacramental church who was unfamiliar with the healing ministry asked whether I thought there was actual healing power in the rites themselves.

My answer was, of course, "no" in the sense that I knew she meant. They are not black magic or a church-instigated form of sorcery. Of themselves, they have no weird healing properties. Essentially, they serve as channels through which God's healing power may flow. They are the means by which we can more easily receive a power infinitely greater than ourselves. As outward and visible signs of God's healing grace, they are an invaluable psychological aid in inspiring faith and arousing hope. For those too weak to pray, they are of incalculable comfort.

A woman who had suffered from a medically diagnosed abdominal cancer recalls: "I couldn't concentrate on prayer, and the effort of summoning up an 'active' faith was just too much. All I could do was 'receive.' When my minister laid on hands, I could virtually feel God's healing peace flow through my body. The pain left, and I fell into a natural sleep within minutes."

This patient was operated on the following day. Although there were clearly discernible evidences of the ravages of cancer, no trace of the malignancy was found. She is today in perfect health.

For those whose conscious minds cannot be reached, such as the insane, the unconscious, and young infants, the healing sacraments have again and again proved of inestimable value.

I recently saw a clergyman anoint an infant reportedly dying from collapsed lungs. The baby was deathly pale and even with the help of oxygen was breathing laboriously. As the minister ended his prayer, the infant stirred. I watched the color creep slowly but unmistakably into her ashen cheeks. The shallow, rapid breathing perceptibly deepened and slowed. She made a complete and rapid recovery.

About six months ago, a minister was called to lay hands on a man in his fifties who had suffered a cerebral hemorrhage. The doctors had warned his family that he could not be expected to regain consciousness before he died. Before the clergyman had lifted his hands from the patient's head, the man opened his eyes in full consciousness, and smiled. Except for a scarcely discernible dragging of his left leg, the patient's recovery has been complete.

A schizophrenic under restraint, whom the doctors called

incurable, was anointed at the request of his family. As the clergyman made the Sign of the Cross on his forehead with the consecrated oil, the patient visibly quieted. His restraints were shortly thereafter removed, and his doctor now offers hope of complete recovery.

Mere chance, you say, that these results should coincide with the administration of the healing rites? I used to think so too, but I have seen too many such cases to write them off as mere coincidences.

The healing work of the Sacraments

So many healings of this sort raise the interesting question as to whether the healing sacraments serve always as mere symbols, mere psychological aids. Could so many seemingly miraculous recoveries be ascribed to a symbol whose meaning a tiny baby, or an unconscious man, or a schizophrenic beyond reason, could not possibly comprehend?

Many theologians of all churches are now in agreement that the sacraments appear to have actual healing power, not of themselves, but according to, and dependent on, the attitude of the person who receives them. Here again, it is a question of faith, somewhere. Obviously patients like the three just mentioned, are incapable of believing anything at all with the conscious mind; but the faith of the Church, or the clergyman, or the attendant family or friends, can supply that belief which is necessary to convert a symbol into an active agent of transforming power—an energy which frequently appears to penetrate into the unconscious or subconscious mind.

Dr. John Ellis Large, who is conducting a notable healing ministry at the Church of the Heavenly Rest in New York City, casts considerable light on the function of the sacramental rites when he says: "I believe that this is a Sacramental universe and that pure spirit is utterly without meaning unless it is incarnate. Even the handshake, the kiss, the pat on the back, takes pure spirit and translates it through our physical bodies."

As the handshake, then, is the physical act by which friendship is expressed, the Sacraments are the physical means by which God's power is conveyed.

These sacramental rites are not essential for healing. It is by simple faith that we reach God, and by earnest prayer that we receive His power in our lives. However, as the Reverend John Gaynor Banks, founder of the Order of St. Luke, has so often emphasized, God is a respecter of *conditions*. Whatever your feeling concerning the actual power inherent in the sacramental acts, it is undeniable that for many they help immeasurably in providing the *occasion* for healing; that they seem to create peculiarly favorable conditions for the operation of the Holy Spirit.

No one church is wholly responsible for the present revival of spiritual healing, but from the beginning the Episcopal Church has led the way. The Reverend Richard Rettig, of St. Peter's United Church of Christ, Pittsburgh, who is himself conducting a remarkable healing ministry, says: "We all owe a tremendous debt to the Episcopal Church, which has demonstrated how the healing ministry could and should be made a part of the normal ministry of every church. As more and more churches are following her lead, Divine healings are no longer exceedingly rare occurrences, but can be *expected* as the result of obedience to Our Lord's Commission."

Clergymen of all denominations have noted the effectiveness of the Episcopal Church—a sacramental church—in the healing field and have eagerly studied her methods. They find them to be based on those of the primitive Church, where healing of the body was considered as vital a church function as the forgiveness of sins. In recognition of the fact that the laying-on-of-hands and anointing are New Testament-authenticated healing techniques, most non-liturgical churches have adopted these same sacramental rites with outstanding results.

Several ministers of non-ritualistic churches to whom I have spoken have expressed concern as to how their congregations, not raised in the sacramental tradition, would accept the sacramental healing methods. A glance at the backgrounds of the communicants attending Episcopal healing services has reassured them; for at most such services members of non-liturgical churches outnumber the Episcopalians. These laymen, as well as their clergy, apparently have no difficulty in accepting the historical precedent of the Sacraments. They recognize in them methods instituted by Our Lord Himself.

Points of contact with God

Spiritual energy, like electric power, is released at a point of contact. The Sacraments seem to serve as extraordinarily strong points of contact with God, through which His divine energy is released in our lives. They make the connection which releases a spiritual light so bright that it may illuminate the soul of a mere bystander who happens to be within its arc.

Take the case of a friend of mine, a newspaper reporter. Last year during Lent he attended a noon service at a downtown church, which, to his surprise, was followed immediately by a healing service.

"I didn't have to be back at my desk for another half hour," he said, "so out of curiosity I decided to stay to find out what this was all about.

"I had never heard of the laying-on-of-hands, and when those who sought healing either for themselves or others, were invited up to the altar rail to receive this rite, I sneaked up to a front pew so as to see better how this, to me definitely peculiar, thing worked. I knelt in the pew so as not to be conspicuous, and watched out of the corner of my eye as the clergyman laid his hands on each head, saying over each supplicant a brief prayer.

"He was only half way down the line when there suddenly rushed through me the strongest conviction I have ever known of the actual Presence of God. For the first time in my life I *knew* beyond the shadow of any doubt that Jesus Christ *was.* This was so profound and exciting an experience that I was unable to return to work. I went home instead to tell my wife what had happened. Since then we've both joined a church for the first time in our lives."

When the Episcopal Church reactivated her healing ministry, dormant for centuries, but always an official part of her ministry, she followed explicitly the healing practice of the primitive Church. Not only does she emphasize the sacramental approach, but, as was also the custom of the early Church, she permits authorized laymen with the gift of healing recognized by St. Paul, (*I Corinthians 12:28*) to work under her supervision. The inspired interdenominational work of such outstanding lay healers as Episcopalian Agnes Sanford and Methodist Louise Eggleston has served to stimulate, encourage, and advance the healing ministry everywhere.

The effectiveness of this combination of charismatic and sacramental healing has been remarked by the clergy of all denominations. As the Reverend Dr. Dixon Rollit, who is conducting an outstanding healing ministry at Pittsburgh's Church of the Ascension, comments: "It is more than mere coincidence that as the use of these New Testament methods increases among our churches, so does the frequency of New Testament-like miracles of spiritual healing." This does not mean that every minister with a healing ministry uses the sacramental rites. There are some, like the Presbyterian pastor, William Holmes, who are conducting most effective ministries without their use.

The laying-on-of-hands

The Reverend Robert Young, also Presbyterian, is more typical of today's healing clergy, when he says: "I always lay on hands. It is a technique authenticated by Our Lord—one that He enjoined His disciples to use."

Mr. Young refers to the fact that the Church derives her authority for this rite from Jesus Christ, who repeatedly laid on hands to heal. "He laid His hands on every one of them, and healed them" (*Luke 4:40*). "And He laid His hands on her: and immediately she was made straight" (*Luke 13:13*). Not only did He use this method Himself, but He charged His disciples to do likewise: "And these signs shall follow them that believe," He said. "In my name shall they cast out devils. . . . They shall lay hands on the sick, and they shall recover" (*Mark 16:17, 18*).

As His hands were the channels of divine healing power, so were the hands of His apostles (*Acts 28:8*), and so are the hands of our healing clergy today. This rite has actually been in continuous use through the centuries as a means of conveying spiritual grace. Not only is it used in Confirmation and Ordination, but at every church service throughout the year; for the outstretched hands of the minister when he pronounces the benediction represent the imposition of hands, which in the early Church was individually administered to each communicant at the close of the service.

Holy Unction

While the laying-on-of-hands is a sacramental act, it may be used by certain spiritually-gifted laymen for healing. Holy Unction, however, is in a slightly different category· Not a sacrament in the sense of the two great Sacraments of Baptism and Holy Communion ordained by Our Lord, Unction is, nevertheless, an official Sacrament of the Church. As such it can be administered only by an ordained minister and received with some degree of preparation. This rite is also a New Testament-authenticated method which obviously had Our Lord's sanction, for under His direction the apostles "cast out many devils and anointed with oil many that were sick, and healed them" (*Mark 6:13*).

St. James actually initiated the format of today's healing

Church when he said, "Is any sick among you? Let him call for the elders of the church; and let them pray over him, anointing with oil in the name of the Lord: And the prayer of faith shall save the sick, and the Lord shall raise him up; and if he have committed sins, they shall be forgiven him" (*James 5:14–15*).

In the early days of the Church, Unction was the Sacrament specifically intended for the healing of the body. It was as a result of the Church's growing failure to heal that the meaning of Unction changed from a healing Sacrament to the rite of Final Absolution.

In an attempt to explain her diminishing healing power, the Church began to teach what Dr. Weatherhead refers to as the "Will of God heresy." This is that God no longer willed to heal and was inflicting suffering and disease as a punishment for sin. As a result, Unction gradually lost its relevance to physical cure and became associated entirely with the forgiveness of sins. Early in the ninth century it became the Extreme Unction of the Roman Church. During the Reformation the Anglican Church officially restored the original use of Unction, but only on paper. It remained an unused and virtually unread portion of the Prayer Book until just a few years ago.

As a better understanding of spiritual healing has developed, and Unction is gradually losing its wide-spread connotation of death, more and more clergymen are reverting to its use. Not only Episcopal priests but a growing number of non-liturgical clergymen report that they regularly use consecrated oil in their healing work. Even the Roman Church has, in individual ministries, re-established the original meaning of the Sacrament, with outstanding healing results.

Some ministers use the rite interchangeably with the laying-on-of-hands, and others use it exclusively. However, most clergymen with very large healing ministries attended by diverse denominations, prefer to administer it only when requested. They think that the meaning of Holy Unction is not yet sufficiently well understood to attempt its use in large, mixed groups. Methodist Dr. Albert Day, who has only recently retired from one of the nation's most outstanding healing ministries, voices the opinion of a number of ministers, when he says: "I found that when Unction was indiscriminately administered to people with no understanding of the Sacrament, it tended to be more of a distraction than a benediction. For this reason, I anoint privately those who desire it."

Both the laying-on-of-hands and Unction have proved to be enormously effective channels for the healing power of the Holy Spirit. However, a good many clergymen report instances of healing which follow anointing, after the imposition of hands has apparently failed.

A man suffering from tuberculosis, for example, had sought healing for many months. While his condition did not worsen, and spiritually he seemed improved, there was no marked change in his physical condition. He finally asked for Unction, and was anointed one morning at ten o'clock. That afternoon was the first in over a year that his temperature did not rise. It remained normal, thereafter; his disease was declared arrested, and he returned to work in an unusually short time.

Another case was that of a woman whose gradually failing eyesight finally resulted in total blindness. Her doctors told her it was hopeless to expect any sort of cure. Believing in Christ's healing power, she received the laying-on-of-hands a number of times, with no apparent result. She was anointed at the altar, at her request. On her way home from the church, she suddenly regained her vision.

Confession

It may well be that the large number of healings which appear to result from Holy Unction are a result of the fact that the rite is so often preceded, at the clergyman's request, by confession. This, too, follows the custom of the early Church, where Unction was the Sacrament for physical cure, while the Sacrament of Penance was intended specifically for the healing of the soul.

The Roman Catholic Church has obligatory Confession; the Episcopal Church offers Sacramental Confession for any who desire it, in addition to the general confession which is provided by every Protestant denomination. As the healing of the body and spirit are interdependent, there seems little doubt that the efficacy of either healing rite is increased by confession, in whatever manner your church provides or your conscience dictates.

God is the healer

One of the great dangers in spiritual healing is the tendency of the patient to identify his healing with the healer instead of with God. The healing then becomes a "faith" cure instead of a spiritual one. This is a particularly great hazard of evangelistic ministries which the sacramental approach helps to avert.

The priest or minister has no personal power. He needs no healing "gift." His only "power" lies in the Holy tradition he represents. He is the dispenser of the Sacraments of the Christian Church purely by virtue of his priesthood and through no virtue of his own. Because his personality does not intrude between the supplicant and God, the true Source of healing is not easily misconstrued.

When the concept of spiritual healing is new to us and someone we know is healed under a particular ministry, even in the church, it is human nature to place great faith in that ministry. I remember, for example, how upset a friend was when the clergyman who had administered to my husband for a heart ailment was unavailable when her own husband suffered a similar illness. But as our understanding of the Sacraments increases, as we feel through them the Power that is "nearer than breathing; closer than hands and feet," we find ourselves gradually "growing out" of faith in a healer into faith in God.

But if the sacramental method helps us to place our eyes on God and not the healer, it can, conversely, lead us into the error of mistaking mere ritual for the road to heaven. The healing rites, indeed Baptism and Holy Communion, can be worthless gestures, meaningless symbols, blind superstition. It is only when they are received with some degree of comprehension, sanctified by faith and activated by prayer, that they become valid, power-charged instruments of the living Christ.

It may be that the sacramental way seems artificial or complicated to you. If it does, don't use it; for it certainly isn't essential. I have confirmed marvelous healings under evangelistic ministries. I have seen wonderful healings occur in churches without benefit of the Sacraments. I have also known remarkable healings to occur at home through prayer. God is always as close to us as the air we breathe. We know the verity of His promise, "Lo, I am with you alway." Yet within His healing Church there is concentrated unprecedented spiritual power. Here most of us can more easily reach out our hands and touch the hem of His garment. Christ came to give us life. Through His body, the Church, and through His arteries, the Sacraments, there is mediated to an extraordinary degree the healing power of the Risen Christ, which throughout the Gospels He has promised us.

Through the ancient rites of healing, used first by Our Lord, our sense of expectancy, our awareness of His love upon which our healing depends, are quickened. Through them our souls and hearts become receptacles for the grace and healing of Jesus Christ. He does not fail to fill them.

CHAPTER 5

Healing for You and Yours— Preparation

$\mathcal{H}$EALING for you and yours is there for the asking. Our Lord said, "Whatsoever ye shall ask the Father in my name, He will give it you" (*John 16:23*). Dare to claim that promise, and you can know its fulfilment.

That there is power in His words believed is not mere surmise. It is a fact as incontestable as that the world is round. You are not treading an unknown way, nor does any burden of proof lie with you. Just as you do not need to prove the efficacy of the wonder drugs, neither do you have to prove the healing power of God. Thousands before you have already done so.

Everyone is worthy of God's healing

A woman said to me the other day: "But who am I to claim His promises? I'm just not good enough to be healed."

Individual worthiness has nothing to do with it. Jesus came
to save sinners, not saints. Your healing is not a reward for
good behavior; it is a fulfilment of His will. No one can
actually be worthy of the redemptive power of Christ. "By
grace are ye saved. . . . It is the gift of God." (*Ephesians
2:8–9*). It is a free gift, rendered us according to our need, by
a God "whose property it is always to have mercy."

If you are a Christian, you must believe that Christ came to
redeem mankind. If you really believe this, you won't find it
difficult to believe that if He still has the power to save your
soul from sin, He also still has the power to heal your body.

No one knows better than I the difficulty of acquiring the
sort of faith which will enable you unreservedly to believe
the words of Our Lord. Yet it can be acquired, and nowhere
else in the realm of human experience is the struggle so worth
the goal. "And He will reward those who diligently seek Him"
is one of the great understatements of the Christian faith.
We are all the children of an infinitely loving and compassionate God. He "came not to judge the world, but to save
the world" (*John 12:47*). He plays no favorites, but "maketh
His sun to rise on the evil and on the good" (*Matthew 5:45*).

A blueprint for action in illness

A short while ago someone asked: "I believe in the will
and power of God to heal, but this is all so new to me. Exactly
what do you *do,* in the event of illness, especially when the
best medical care seems unavailing?"

This is so common a question that to answer it I will blue-
print a course of action which has proved enormously effective
in scores of cases.

If you are physically able, attend healing services at a
church. No matter how slight your knowledge or how small
your belief, your presence in a church is a demonstrable act
of faith on your part which Our Lord will honor. It is no longer
necessary to travel to one of the great shrines, such as Lourdes,

for *every* healing church is now a shrine, consecrated by the prayers of the faithful and hallowed by the presence of the Holy Spirit. In the fellowship of believers, in the atmosphere of expectant trust which pervades the healing church, you will find your own faith fortified and sustained, and you will grow in grace and understanding.

But the healing power of Christ is by no means confined to the altars of His Church. If you are physically unable to go to church, contact several churches with healing ministries, asking each one to pray for your healing. The illimitable power of corporate prayer is not conjectural, it is established fact. Although all prayer is beneficial, the prayers of those, clergy and laity alike, who uncompromisingly believe that God can and will cure the sick, have a unique healing power.

Next, if you or the patient is familiar with, and sympathetic to, the healing sacraments, ask for the laying-on-of-hands or Unction. If it is possible, notify a prayer group at what hour the sacramental rites are to be administered. Their prayers, offered simultaneously with yours and those of the officiating clergyman, will have tremendous power.

This power was demonstrated in the healing of a man with a carefully diagnosed stomach cancer. The patient's wife had been told by his doctors that one-third of his stomach would have to be removed. She had also been warned that owing to a serious heart condition her husband's chance of survival was extremely slim.

It was arranged that the patient receive the laying-on-of-hands an hour before surgery. A healing prayer group was so notified, and their prayers requested. The patient was wheeled to the operating room, serene and unafraid.

The surgeon found no trace of cancer. All evidence of the heart ailment had disappeared. "Only a Higher Power could have caused this healing," was the comment of the doctor. This healing occurred four years ago, and there has been no return of any symptoms.

If a patient is unfamiliar with the healing rites and might

be either antagonistic to or frightened by their administration, the laying-on-of-hands may be received by others with special intention for the sick one. Such was the case of a physicist with a lung cancer diagnosed by X-ray, sputum analysis, and bronchoscope. Prayers for his recovery were offered by many different churches, and at least one novena was made.

On a certain Thursday morning at ten A.M. an entire prayer group attended, as a body, a healing service, receiving the laying-on-of-hands on behalf of the ill scientist. "Within an hour of this service," the erstwhile patient reports, "something strange happened to me. I was suddenly flooded with an ecstasy of joy. I felt a keen awareness of the actual Presence of God in my room, accompanied with a conviction that I would recover."

The anticipated surgery in this case was never undertaken, for all subsequent laboratory tests proved negative. The patient was able to resume work in a week, and has had no recurrence of symptoms after a period of three years.

Healing depends on you

But as important as are corporate and intercessory prayer, and as effective as is the receiving of the healing rites, the release of the full power of the healing Christ in your life depends on you and your ability or at least your attempt to meet certain conditions. Spiritual healing is filled with paradoxes. Miracles are wrought by faith, yet faith is often born through miracles. Spiritual regeneration effects physical healing, yet sometimes the physical healing occurs first. The spiritual change immediately follows as a result.

Some people are healed by faith alone, with no prior preparation; yet there is a great fundamental truth of spiritual healing which cannot be over-emphasized. Indeed, if there were but one key to God's healing power, this might well be it. It is your willingness to remain unhealed physically, if you can only know God. Nowhere is it more clearly illustrated than in spiritual healing that "Whosoever will save his life shall lose it: but whosoever will lose his life for my sake, the same shall save it" (*Luke 9:24*).

This is not an easy concept. To one who is in pain, the cessation of pain may seem to take precedence over everything else. When a loved one appears to be hopelessly ill, his physical recovery can seem the only thing that matters. Your belief that the soul's salvation is more important than the body's healing, can be acquired only by the help of God through prayer. If you are like most of us, it will be impossible for you continually to sustain this conviction. It will most probably come to you as a sudden revelation. It may not last, but that flash of truth is sufficient to cause a miracle.

It did in the case of a West Pointer doomed to live out his life as a cripple in continual pain from a shattered leg which repeated surgery had failed to heal. "As I received the laying-on-of-hands," he said, "I suddenly knew that the only thing that really mattered was that I find God. All at once the pain in my leg and the fact that my doctors had told me I'd never walk again without crutches, didn't seem to matter at all."

Within two days after this experience, he was completely without pain and was walking unassisted on the injured leg. He walks today with no sign of a limp. "This healing is the work of God," reports his stupefied orthopedic surgeon.

The wife of a business executive reports a similar experience. "I had been told by my husband's doctors that he could not recover from a grave kidney ailment. My husband didn't believe in spiritual healing, so I'd wait until he was asleep at night, then gently lay my hands on him and pray. My own faith was very weak, and all that seemed to matter was that his death somehow, some way, be staved off. Then one morning at about two A.M. I had a sudden flash of revelation that both he and I were closer to God than we had ever been before. I knew, for just a split second, the complete joy of standing on what seemed the threshhold of His Kingdom. I experienced a sense of total conviction that death could never separate my husband and myself.

I slept then, and awoke for the first time in days without fear. My husband's condition dramatically changed for the better. Today, three years later, he is in perfect health."

Time and again it has been demonstrated that our best assurance of healing lies in the fullness of our realization that God's greatest gift to us is Himself. Unless we seek Him for His own sake, and not for His healing power, we may well be denied both.

Trust in God casts out fear

A woman with a seriously ill child remarked to me not long ago, "Everywhere in the healing ministry I hear people referring to the 'prayer of faith.' I wonder precisely what they mean. I believe that God can heal my little girl, but if I'm supposed to pray without fear, I might as well not pray at all. I can't *help* being afraid."

Neither can countless others who worry needlessly that fear will block the inflow of God's healing power. If human fear impeded healing, there would be today very little evidence of the operation of the Holy Spirit. While obviously we should have that complete trust in God which would cast out all fear, few of us do have it. But as Our Lord in His mercy understands our struggle for faith, so does He in His compassion comprehend our anxiety for those we love.

As for the "prayer of faith" it is a simple thing. It is talking to God as you would talk to your own earthly father, with implicit trust in His love for you and unfaltering confidence in His personal concern for your welfare. It is knowing in your heart what you say with your lips.

It is generally conceded that faith and the intellect have nothing to do with one another. Yet I have found that, for most of us, our minds must be reasonably satisfied with the concept of the healing Christ before we can take that final step which leads to our heart's acceptance of Him. The prayer resulting from the reconciliation of our mind's belief and our heart's faith is the means by which His power is set free in our lives.

Reconciliation with God

How can you effect this reconciliation? Give Him just thirty minutes a day of your time, and He will do the rest. He is only waiting for you to take that one step, however tentative, in His direction. His outstretched Hands are ready to clasp yours.

Select a time and place where you can be relaxed and undisturbed. At night, in bed, is a particularly good time, for then the subconscious can take over when you sleep. Begin by reading one of the accounts of healing in the Gospels (listed at the end of this book), for this is one of the surest methods of discovering and believing the healing Christ. "Faith cometh by hearing, and hearing by the word of God" (*Romans 10:17*). Listen well, so that you may know exactly what it is you seek. In our anxiety to acquire faith, we often confuse faith with its object, mistaking the means for the end. We speak of "healing by faith," but it is not faith which heals. It is Jesus Christ. No one was ever healed by his own laboriously achieved belief.

As you read, note how clear a distinction Our Lord makes between involuntary sickness and disease, which He so often refers to as "works of the devil," and voluntary suffering, or the bearing of the cross for His sake. You cannot help seeing the emphasis he places on physical healing. The implication of healing with the Kingdom and the interrelationship of the two cannot escape you.

"And He sent them to preach the kingdom of God, and to heal the sick" (*Luke 9:2*).

"Heal the sick . . . and say unto them, The kingdom of God is come nigh unto you" (*Luke 10:9*).

"And as ye go, preach, saying, The kingdom of heaven is at hand. Heal the sick, . . . raise the dead, cast out devils" (*Matthew 10:7–8*).

"If I with the finger of God cast out devils, no doubt the kingdom of God is come upon you" (*Luke 11:20*).

Reflect for a moment on these statements. Has God changed His mind about what constitutes the kingdom? If so, then He is a changeable God, *not* the same yesterday, today, and forever. Has Jesus, the Christ, lost His desire and capacity to heal? If so, then He has withdrawn His commission to His Church to "preach the Gospel to every creature. . . . lay hands on the sick, and they shall recover" (*Mark 16:15, 18*). I think you will agree that this is a highly irrational assumption.

How to banish doubts

At this point, if you have any lingering doubts as to God's will to heal you, bring them out in the open and face them. Ask yourself what may seem an irrelevant question: Do you believe in doctors? Haven't you always tried to obtain the best medical care for your family and yourself? If your answer is in the affirmative, and at the same time you question God's will to heal you, you have presented yourself with an irreconcilable inconsistency. Do you honestly believe that you are going against the will of God when you consult your doctor? Do you really believe that all hospitals, doctors, and nurses are flouting His will in their battle against disease and suffering? In the obvious answer to this question, I believe you will find your answer to what God wills for you.

Now consider some of the many promises He made you: "He that believeth on me, the works that I do shall he do also; and greater works than these shall he do; because I go unto my Father" (*John 14:12*). "If we ask any thing according to His will, He heareth us" (*I John 5:14*). "Ask, and it shall be given you; seek and ye shall find; knock, and it shall be opened unto you" (*Luke 11:9*).

Consider whether you believe *anything* that Christ said in the Gospels. If you do, why should you disbelieve the promises He made you? Remind yourself how unthinkingly you place your trust in those around you. If your bank promises three per cent interest on your savings, don't you believe it? If your grocer promises delivery of your order in time for dinner, don't you believe him? If a friend promises to do an errand for you, don't you assume that he will keep his word? Is Jesus Christ less reliable than your banker or your grocer or a casual friend?

Shut the door of your mind now, and silently repeat: "Be still, and know that I am God" (*Psalms 46:10*).

"They that wait upon the Lord shall renew their strength" (*Isaiah 40:31*).

"All things are yours" (*I Corinthians 3:21*).

Rest now for a moment in the comfort of the greatest of all His promises, which you are already beginning to realize: "I shall never leave thee nor forsake thee. . . . Lo, I am with you alway, even unto the end of the world" (*Matthew 28:20*).

Don't worry about your faith, or try to compute it. If you have come this far in an effort to find the healing Christ, you are already within His touch; for "ye shall . . . find me, when ye shall search for me with all your heart" (*Jeremiah 29:13*).

The door of your soul is opening. God is entering in.

You are ready now to pray your healing prayer.

CHAPTER 6

Healing for You and Yours—
Healing Prayer

*W*ALK with firm steps to the throne of God. Ask for your healing, not hesitantly nor shyly, but boldly and positively. Remember that you are aligning yourself with God against the forces of evil. You are affirming His will. Do it in a strong, courageous manner.

If you pray for yourself, ask forgiveness for those sins of which you are guilty. Make as certain as you can that your contrition is honest, that you are sorry, not because your sin is hurting you by blocking you from God's benefits, but because your sin is hurting Christ.

Praying for others

If you pray for another, quietly repeat the name of the person for whom you seek healing. It is important that you visualize the patient entirely well, completely whole, vibrant with His life. If your prayer is for a loved one, ask that Christ's power cleanse the patient of resentment, hostility, hatred, false pride and all other sin.

Visualize Our Lord in the sick room, laying His Hands on the patient; or, if you prefer, mentally hold the patient up to God for healing.

"Let Your healing Light flood every organ of this body; your Love permeate its every cell," might form the basis for your prayer. "Fortify my faith, Oh Lord, strengthen my trust in thee. In the Name of Jesus Christ, I ask and claim this healing."

Use any words you wish. The important thing is to ask and to be confident of His will, for by confidence your faith is released. Ask, expecting the healing, for by your expectancy, His power is liberated.

Whatever else you do, make sure to end your prayer with thanksgiving for the healing, believing it already accomplished. This conviction of victory, even before it is ostensibly realized, is the essence of all faith and prayer, and the root of Christian healing. "As thou hast believed, so be it done unto thee" (*Matthew 8:13*). Jesus has left us no room for speculation on this point, which He so dramatically illustrated at the tomb of Lazarus. You recall His great prayer of faith while Lazarus *still lay dead:* "Father, I thank thee that thou hast heard me" (*John 11:41*).

Our Lord did not wait until Lazarus was restored to life before He prayed His thanks. As certainly as He gave us the Lord's Prayer, so did the Son of God give us the key to healing when He said, "What things soever ye desire, when ye pray, believe that ye receive them, and ye shall have them" (*Mark 11:24*).

To believe you have received before you see the evidence is the crux of faith. It is one of God's conditions, not only for healing, but for all His blessings.

This sort of faith is progressive. It can be cultivated through prayer. It increases as your awareness of the reality of the healing Christ grows. Conversely, your awareness of Him quickens through increased faith—a faith which gradually accepts the promise that "with God all things are possible"— and goes courageously forth to claim it.

Conclude your prayer with praise for the victory, "being fully persuaded that, what He had promised, He was able also to perform" (*Romans 4:21*). Thank God, knowing that you are healed.

Pray your healing prayer. Then commit the patient to God, convinced of His healing will and loving care. A common tendency, when we are worried about someone close to us, is to repeat endlessly: "God, please heal him." Prodding God's memory with parrot-like repetition is not necessary; it does not constitute a power-filled healing prayer. Pray your prayer once a day, and leave the patient in God's Hands.

To believe that you have received healing before it is evident does not mean that you should stop praying. In all but one of the recorded New Testament miracles, the healings were instantaneous. I have seen many marvelous instant healings, but today the majority are gradual. The faith of the Church as a whole is still weak, and the spiritual stature of most of us is still small. If you are not healed at once, continue your daily devotions. Attend healing services faithfully, and receive the sacramental healing rites at regular intervals. As you grow in understanding, and as your spiritual perception quickens, you can expect your physical ailment to respond to His great healing power.

Jesus said that "men must always pray and not give up" (*Luke 18:1*, Goodspeed). I have on file many cases like that of a World War II veteran who, according to medical opinion, had been hopelessly and permanently crippled by a landmine explosion. He began to attend the weekly healing services in his local church seven years ago. It was nearly four years before his physical healing was complete.

God hears all prayers

A great many people say that they find it difficult, if not impossible, to pray for themselves. A man suffering from extreme hypertension put it like this: "I feel guilty praying for myself, there are so many worse off than I am." This is a typical reaction which all of us may share to some extent. Being human, we tend to limit God. We're afraid that if we "bother" Him by asking healing for ourselves, we'll cheat others who may need Him more.

But the greatness of God cannot be confined to our human concepts. His Presence and power are limitless and indivisible. To each one of us who seek Him, He is *wholly* there in His full majesty and power. When we accept Him in our hearts, we receive the full God. We are depriving no one else. Just as television brings simultaneously to millions the same picture, the same personality, the same voice, so is God present simultaneously to every individual in the whole world.

Therefore, in the case of our own illness, we should attempt to pray for ourselves as best we can.

Bishop Austin Pardue comments: "I feel very sorry for anyone who does not consistently seek help from the Lord. The person who does not pray for himself is missing contact with the source of all power."

We will find additional help in asking the prayers of others. Most of all we will be aided by attending healing services. We will discover at the altar of our church that it is no more difficult to receive the sacramental rites for our physical healing than to receive Holy Communion for our spiritual regeneration.

Fasting

Numerous people wonder about fasting in connection with healing. Fasting and prayer have always gone hand in hand. Jesus used it in His healing work (*Mark 9:29*), and there is frequent reference to fasting in connection with the healing ministry of the early-post-apostolic Church. The value of fasting in today's healing ministry has been demonstrated again and again. As an act of faith which quickens us spiritually, it makes us vastly more receptive to the Holy Spirit. It is certainly to be recommended before attending a healing service.

A young woman whose father (a medical doctor) suffered a serious ailment of his left eye decided to accompany her prayers for his recovery with an all-day fast. Prior to this decision both she and her father had prayed and attended healing services with no discernible physical result.

Late in the afternoon of the day she was fasting she was seized with an intolerably severe pain over her left eye. "It got so bad," she relates, "that I vowed I'd never fast again. At the end of an hour I was ready to give up and get something to eat, convinced that hunger was causing the headache. Then suddenly the pain stopped."

Unknown to her, at the time of the onset of her pain, her father was sitting in an ophthalmologist's office, awaiting a final examination before surgery on his eye. Suddenly he felt his diseased eye begin to water copiously. When the eye was examined twenty minutes later, no sign of the ailment remained.

Share the glad tidings

Because I believe that one of the great divine purposes of today's manifestation of the healing power is conversion; because I have seen the first faint glimmerings of faith so often fanned into flame by the witness of those healed, I believe that it is incumbent upon those who have felt His healing touch, to bear witness.

"And the things that thou hast heard of me among many witnesses, the same commit thou to faithful men, who shall be able to teach others also" (*II Timothy* 2:2).

But witness with care. Don't make careless claims of divine

healing. Don't talk incessantly of what God has done for you, or you place yourself in the same category as the bore who talks of nothing but his operation. With dignity and circumspectness, do as He asked: show "how great things God hath done unto thee" (*Luke* 8:39).

Probably through the witness of others you yourself found the healing Christ. Don't withhold the great truth you have discovered.

"If ye continue in my word, then are ye my disciples indeed" (*John* 8:31). As such, and with deep concern for the spiritual welfare of others, share the glad tidings.

The power of Jesus' name

A few months ago a woman asked me: "Suppose someone is taken suddenly and violently ill, say, with a heart attack. Suppose that you believe in the power of God to heal, but know practically nothing of spiritual healing, and are in no way prepared to pray a powerful prayer of faith. What can you do?"

I answered her with the story of a woman whose husband had recently suffered a coronary attack. It was his second attack, and because of the severe heart damage resulting from the first, suffered three years before, the cardiologist had predicted that another such attack could well prove fatal.

"Tom woke me about three A.M. gasping for breath, sweat pouring down his face from the awful pain in his chest and elbows. I was much too frightened to pray a real prayer; but while I was waiting for the doctor, I knelt by my husband and placed my hands lightly on his chest. Then I seemed instinctively to make the Sign of the Cross while I repeated the words; 'In the name of Jesus, let him be healed.' Almost at once his pain diminished and he grew less fearful. By the time the doctor arrived a few minutes later, Tom seemed remarkably like himself. The doctor sent him to the hospital where oxygen and emergency medication would be at hand. The next day heart X-rays and a series of cardiograms were ordered. Not only did the new lab tests indicate no additional damage—there was no evidence of the original infarction!"

So many cases of this nature have given rise to the question: "Is there actual power in the Name of Christ?" In the middle of the twentieth century this seems a fantastic idea. Yet so impressive has been evidence of this power that a group of scientists in England, headed by several eminent British doctors including a well-known Roman Catholic surgeon, have engaged in experimental studies in which they claim to have demonstrated that when the Name of Jesus Christ and the Sign of the Cross are used in healing, a marked and instantaneous difference in the radiations emanating from the patient's body can be detected.

That there should be actual power in the Name of Christ is not so incredible as it appears at first glance, when we realize that today's healing ministry is based so closely on the New Testament and early post-apostolic Church methods, with many of the same results. We are told by St. Luke that "the seventy returned again with joy, saying, Lord, even the devils are subject unto us through Thy Name" (*Luke 10:17*).

In the writings of the Church Fathers in the second and third centuries, there is repeated reference to the "power in the Name"; the fact that "The Name of Jesus taketh away disease" (*Origen*).

To anyone who has closely observed the healing ministry at work today, this same power is clearly discernible. Obviously it does not lie in meaningless repetition of a word which may induce a sort of hypnosis. Nor does it reside in the vain reiteration of a syllable, utilized as a kind of magic incantation. The power in the Name is in its use as an outward expression of our inward (and perhaps subconscious) acceptance of Him as the source of all love, all life, and all power. All the spiritual preparation I have suggested is that you may know this truth with your heart. This is all you need to know to find the healing Christ.

The stones in the structure of your faith are your conviction that God wills your health; that physical healing is as much a part of Our Lord's ministry of salvation today as when He walked the earth; and that God's promises are meant for *you*. Their realization depends only on your courage to claim them for yourself.

Remember that "All things are possible to him that believeth" (*Mark 9:23*).

Remember that it is in your quest for God, and your hunger for His Kingdom, that you will find the healing Christ.

Above all, remember this: You were saved by Our Lord on the Cross. You have only to receive and claim that salvation. He, long ago, made you a promise: "If ye shall ask anything in my name, I will do it."

Ask now, in the Name of Jesus, for your healing. He will honor your faith.

CHAPTER 7

How to Stay Well

$\mathcal{I}$T IS an infinitely wonderful thing to be healed by
the power of God, but it is even more wonderful to remain
well.

Most of us tend to seek God's healing power only when we
and our doctors are at the end of our ropes. This use of the
healing ministry makes it a ministry of desperation, of last
resort, which it should not be.

As far as physical healing is concerned, you should seek
God's help at the onset of illness. You should not hesitate to
call your clergyman when sickness strikes, any more than to
call your doctor. Time and time again there have been remarkable results when the medical profession and the clergy
work concurrently—not only in cases of dire illness such as
cancer or tuberculosis or a severe coronary, but in less dramatic ailments.

Take, for example, the case of a young man with a severe stomach ulcer, whose doctor had prescribed two weeks of hospitalization, and six months of drastically curtailed activity. Immediately after the diagnosis of ulcer was made, the patient received the laying-on-of-hands with prayer. After six days in the hospital, X-rays showed the ulcer completely healed.

Or take the case of a woman with a torn muscle in her arm, whose orthopedist placed the limb in a cast for two weeks, advising that at the end of this time, an intensive program of therapy, exercise, and massage would be necessary. Prayers were immediately held, and the laying-on-of-hands administered. When the cast was removed, the arm was perfectly well, and no further treatment was indicated.

Healing of nervous and emotional difficulties are also greatly expedited by the cooperation of medicine and clergy, as in the case of a young woman suffering from a profound nervous exhaustion, who was literally too tired to raise her arms to comb her hair. Her neurologist's prognosis: recovery would take at least a year of rest and treatment. The outcome after attending four healing services with a friend: a complete return to her former energetic self within a month.

Mistaken medical prognoses? Sheer coincidence? Doctors familiar with spiritual healing no longer think so. "We are beginning to realize," says Dr. Burnett Rae, "that spiritual healing is not an additional form of therapy to be tried when all else has failed, but is central to the whole problem of health and healing."

Spiritual healing not for sick alone

Because the ministry of healing is essentially spiritual in character, it is not just for the sick. It is for all who seek an inpouring of the Holy Spirit; for all who want to know Christ better and to love Him more; for all in search of peace of mind, and that rare spiritual treasure, peace of soul; for all who seek that abundant life He came to bring us.

Countless seekers have found the object of their search at the altar of the healing church. Just why there should be so vivid an awareness of the reality of Christ through the healing sacraments is a phenomenon that defies explanation. Yet that He is overwhelmingly present in the healing church is apparent to even the unbeliever.

Not long ago while walking with an electronics engineer, we passed a church well known for its healing ministry. I asked him to go in with me for a moment. He was a complete skeptic, but he reluctantly agreed.

No service was in progress, and the church was entirely empty. We sat in a back pew for a few moments, in silence. Then the man turned to me and said, with excitement in his voice: "There's some strange power in here. I can feel it, like electricity. What is there in this church?" The answer to that question? Christianity.

So impregnated with power is the healing church that it is not at all unusual for healing to occur while a patient prays in an edifice devoid of minister or congregation, but full of the Holy Spirit.

If a healing of cancer or diabetes can occur in an empty church by virtue of the Holy Spirit, it is not strange that our nervous tensions, anxieties and fatigue are successfully dissolved by this same recreating power so abundantly in evidence during a healing service.

Healing services strengthen faith

For most of us, the battle for faith is a continuing one—the price we pay to reach His throne. I remember when a clergyman with an outstanding healing ministry said to me: "You know, for months after I had started healing services, I had to fight for faith. Even now, although I have seen many miracles of healing, my subconscious and conscious minds still occassionally war. But each time I lay on hands, I feel again the full impact of His Presence."

In my own case, even after I had seen with my own eyes and had had verified such marvelous evidence of God's healing power, I would often go home and feel the faith literally drain out of me. Often it was not fully restored until I went again to a healing service. It is through the inspiration of the healing church and the massed faith of believers that our own faith is inevitably strengthened and rekindled. Indeed it is even born, if the desire for faith is there.

But the healing ministry does more than revive our faltering faith. Because of the tangible evidence it provides that God lives today; because of the demonstrable proof it offers that He is a God of mercy and love, who relieves our suffering whether mental, physical, or spiritual, the teaching of His Son acquires for us a new relevance and validity. We gain a new and thrilling insight into all the aspects of His ministry. We are aware at last of the vast difference between knowing *about* Our Lord, and knowing *Him*. The historical Jesus has become for us the living, pulsating Christ, who metamorphoses our lives.

Illumined by new knowledge, the Gospel of Our Lord is revealed in all its power. We recognize, as surely as did the apostles and the early Christians, the good news brought us by the Son of God: that He came not to save bodies and not to save souls, but to save men. We know the truth at last, and the truth has indeed set us free.

Because the radiance of the healing Christ has cast a new light of comprehension over all of Christianity, we are able to receive the *full* faith, through which we are assured we may inherit all His promises (*Hebrews 6:12*).

Healing power in Baptism and Communion

Take, for example, the tremendous healing power inherent in two great Sacraments ordained by Our Lord, Baptism and Holy Communion. Our awareness of the living, healing Christ has transformed these often casually received rites into instruments of breath-taking regenerative power—physical as well as spiritual.

We find that "Be baptized . . . and ye shall receive the gift of the Holy Spirit" is not an idle promise of indiscernible spiritual benefit. We note that scores of adults have received healing after the administration of this Sacrament.

The Reverend Edgar Sanford, with a healing ministry of long duration, has baptized many critically sick infants, for whom no hope of recovery was held. Not one of these baptized babies died.

So many healings have followed the administration of the Sacrament of Holy Communion, although it is not a specific healing rite, as to suggest that it may actually be the greatest of all healing Sacraments. When the Lord's Supper is received with a fuller understanding of the healing Christ and the totality of His redemptive mission, it takes on a new and profound significance. It becomes fraught with the power of His redeeming Presence—the power which heals both body and soul.

Our Lord's assurance that "He that eateth my flesh, and drinketh my blood, dwelleth in me, and I in him" (*John 6:56*) takes on a new trenchancy as we realize that through Holy Communion we and His whole Church receive not only the "remission of sins and all other benefits of His passion" (*Book of Common Prayer, page 81*), but His Incarnate Life.

Our personal relationship with God is the most vital of all our relationships. It demands much the same expenditure of time and effort on our parts as the establishment and maintenance of our human relationships. To *make* friends, for example, we must spend time with people so that we may learn really to know them. To keep friends, we must exert the effort to visit with them, or we lose contact and our sense of closeness with them. So it is with God. The aim and purpose of spiritual healing, is to build our lives in harmony with His will. Prayer and meditation are the means by which we learn to know God better and achieve this harmony.

Prayer maintains health

How, through God, can you remain well? How can you be free from physical disease and free from the tensions and harassments which beset most of us in these times? If prayer is a vital factor in healing, it is equally vital in maintaining full and vibrant health.

Donald Robertson, M.D., writes in a recent article in *The Christian Century*: "Prayer promotes maturity and eliminates neuroses and neurotic behavior. When we surrender our lives to God, the old physical machine can turn off its defenses. Blood pressure drops, digestion is re-established, tensions dissolve, and normal sleep returns. That is why I, as a physician, assign such an important place to prayer in relationship to the problem of health."

Many of us have long dismissed the "practice of the Presence of God" as a spiritual exercise indulged in only by the cloistered religious. But no matter how religiously illiterate you may be, when you have once felt this Presence at a healing service, you will no longer be content without it. The Kingdom has already been planted in your heart.

Meditation will no longer seem the pastime of a few religious, but the means of bringing Him into your life so that you will know the exaltation of His continued nearness.

Daily prayer will no longer consist of a hasty ritual, mumbled before you fall asleep. It will be the treasured means by which you can learn to know and experience God—the means by which His power is released in your life, and by which He enters in.

What, you may wonder, will be the factual results of His Presence in your life? Here are some: you will never again know loneliness; your fears and your anxieties will disappear, for they cannot coexist with the living Christ. In Him and through Him, you will find as He promised, the "peace which passeth all understanding."

Praying effectively

How do you meditate and pray? There is no single way, but here is one which is simple and effective:

The first thing to do is to delegate a portion of time each day for quiet devotions. Whether it is fifteen minutes or an hour or two, observe it every day.

Start with a comparatively short period every day, increasing it as you may desire. This is better psychologically than to set aside a large segment of time, and find yourself gradually decreasing it until you may omit it altogether.

For the sake of convenience, divide your devotional period into two sections, one of meditation and one of prayer.

Begin the first part by relaxing comfortably in a chair. Close your eyes, and try to realize that you are in God's Presence. Repeat, aloud or silently, one or more of the following texts: "Be still my soul" or "My strength is in thy might" or "I shall not fear" or "Lord, increase my faith" or "My peace I give unto you." Say these words slowly, thinking carefully about what you are saying.

Now read one chapter from the New Testament. Read consecutively so that in time you will have read the entire New Testament. In this way you will learn to know better the mind of God.

Read slowly a psalm such as the Twenty-third, which will increase your inner peace; or the Ninety-first, which will add to your trust. Throughout your reading, stop at intervals, and contemplate His nearness to you, remembering His words: "If a man love me . . . my Father will love him, and we will come unto him, and make our abode with him" (*John 14:23*). Let the sense of His abiding presence wash over you.

Realize that you are always in the presence of God, for God

is everywhere. Nevertheless you will have to *know* that you are in His presence before His power becomes available to you. This meditative, contemplative approach helps you to know; therefore devote as much time as you can to it, but not so much that your attention begins to wander. Even the few minutes spent as I have suggested, if persisted in daily, will increase your consciousness of God to the point that you know that He *is*, and that Christ dwells in your heart. Your spiritual perception will be quickened, and that spark of the divine which is in you will be released with remarkable results in your life.

Much as I dislike the word "technique" in connection with prayer, it is undeniable that there is a technique that when followed achieves results.

In addition to the Lord's Prayer (which should be said every day) there are other specific kinds of prayer. The prayer of faith for healing is not the same as the prayer for guidance, through which we strive to learn His will. The prayer of worship is different from the contemplative prayer in which we attempt to enter the Presence.

A *framework for prayer*

For those who want to pray, but are not sure how; or for those who have prayed for years but would like to pray more effectively, I suggest the following framework, which includes the five essential points of prayer. By daily adherence to this general pattern, you can realize in your life the illimitable power of prayer.

1. ADORATION: Begin your prayer by a recognition of the Holiness of God. A great physiologist says: "The most ignored mental activity which gives strength to personality, and power to prayer, is a sense of the Holy: this God so approachable to him who knows how to love is hidden from him who knows only how to understand."

All prayer should begin, as does the model prayer, in an

atmosphere of reverence and love. To worship and to love is an instinctive human need. You will not find it difficult to worship your God. "Hallowed be thy Name." Repeat this phrase slowly. Then follow it with "Praise ye the Lord" or "Praise the Lord, O my soul, and all that is within me" or "Holy, Holy, Holy, Lord God of Hosts. Heaven and earth are full of thy glory."

2. CONFESSION or PENITENCE: You are in the Presence of God, of complete holiness. Ask Him, with humility, for forgiveness and believe that you receive it. You have been told on good authority that a contrite heart is the only requisite for absolution.

3. INTERCESSION: Intercessory prayer has been called the purest form of prayer. Bishop Everett Jones aptly terms it, "Love on its knees." Here you are holding up to God, for His help and healing, those who are sick or oppressed. Pray for those close to you whom you love, and ask that they go their ways, continually surrounded and protected by the might and love of Christ.

Then pray for the sick in mind, body, and spirit all over the world, asking that the healing hands of Christ be unfettered by the power of believing prayer. Pray that this power shall be realized in its full glory, unimpeded by doubt and unweakened by skepticism, touching all who are in need. End your intercession with a prayer for the belief of the unbelieving Church. For when the full faith of the whole Church is universally restored, the Kingdom will be clearly discernible, and we will know a foretaste of heaven.

4. PETITION: We come now to the time when we may voice our own needs to God. For many of us, this has been the first and last prayer we have ever learned. While there is, of course, a definite place for our personal petitions, if we make this our *only* prayer, perpetually bombarding God with our personal demands, the result tends to be negative. When we keep our petitionary prayer in its proper context as one of the points to be covered in the prayer pattern, but not the only one,

then it has power. When we pray carefully, certain that what we ask is not in conflict with His will and confident that Christ knows and understands our needs, whether they be physical, material or spiritual, we may expect fulfilment of our requests.

5. GRATITUDE: Express now, as well as upon awakening and upon going to bed and continually throughout the day, your gratitude to God for those countless blessings He has bestowed upon you. Your wife, your husband, your children, your sight, your hearing, your health, a good meal, a lovely day. There is never a time that you cannot find something for which to be grateful. Even if things seem to have piled up on you and you feel depressed wondering what on earth you have to be thankful *for*, you can at least offer thanks that things are not always so bad!

Let your gratitude be the underlying theme of your life. Let your thanksgiving for God; for His sacrifice for you on the Cross; for His forgiveness; for His intercession for you and yours, be the keynote of your worship.

St. Paul says: "In everything give thanks: for this is the will of God" (*I Thessalonians 5:18*). If you *do* make sincere thankfulness a way of life, you will find that something wonderful happens. You will have set in motion an infallible law of prayer. Your blessings will be added to in direct proportion to your gratitude for those already received. "Metaphysicians have discovered," writes Charles Fillmore, "that words that express thanks, gratitude, and praises, release energies of mind and soul; and their use is usually followed by effects so pronounced that they are quickly identified with the words that provoke them." Say these words with your lips and mean them in your heart, and you will prove the verity of this statement.

End your devotions with a short period of silence. For prayer is communion with God, not a monologue. You have talked to Him; now let Him speak to you. You are likely to find that you have never heard Him until now, not because He hasn't spoken, but because you haven't listened.

Your formal daily devotions are over, but your prayers are not. "Pray without ceasing" is the injunction of St. Paul. You will find that brief mental invocations throughout the day, such as "Holy, Holy, Holy" or "I laud and magnify thy Holy Name," or "Thanks be to God," are sufficient to hold you in His Presence. Say these or similar short prayers on the bus, or in the office or at home, bearing in mind that this is not to remind God of *you*, but you of *God*.

You will find, as have so many others, that you will grow into prayer by praying, and come into the Presence through practice.

The actual words you say are immaterial. All that really matters is what is in your heart. God recognizes your slightest impulse toward Him through prayer, and honors it. Your attempt, however feeble it may be in the beginning, to link yourself with His inexhaustible power will result in the restoration of your spirit and in the strengthening of your body. You will know at last, from personal experience, the full meaning of these words: "They that wait upon the Lord shall renew their strength; they shall mount up with wings as eagles; they shall run, and not be weary; and they shall walk, and not faint" (*Isaiah 40:31*).

Physical benefits from prayer

The spiritual benefits of prayer have long been known but it is largely through the healing ministry that we have become aware of its physical results. As long as there is sin in the world, there will be sickness. It is interesting to note, however, the improvement in health and the unusual maintenance of good health enjoyed by those associated with the healing ministry, either as laymen or clergymen. A Presbyterian attorney who became interested in the healing ministry some two years ago, voices the experience of innumerable people when he says: "I had all my life been subject to severe colds, throat infections, and sinus trouble during the winter months. I am convinced that it is more than coincidence that during the past two years I have not been indisposed, even for a day."

The experience of a mother with three youngsters is also typical. "For years I have been nervous and tired," she says, "and also terribly apprehensive about the children's health. But not any more. Through the healing ministry I have an entirely different concept of God. I know now that He wants them to be well, and that if they do get sick, He will heal them. The result has been that they have turned into the healthiest youngsters on our block, practically never have even colds. As for me, the days aren't long enough to do all I want to do. I sleep like a top and have forgotten what 'nerves' mean."

Realization of the healing Christ transforms our lives. It eradicates our fears, for we know that in His mercy, He will protect and heal us. It dispels our anxieties, for we know that in His compassion, He will guide us to a solution of our problems. It dissipates our tensions, for we know that we can unequivocally trust Him.

Confident of His love for us, we can rest and relax in the greatness of God. At last we have learned the joy of Christianity. "Joy to the world, the Lord has come," is no longer merely the opening line of a familiar hymn. It is a reality imbedded in our hearts. Joy invariably induces a salubrious physical reaction. Couple it with a sense of security in a God who cares; confidence in a God who heals; assurance in a God who protects; and jittery nerves, worry, and fear will be a thing of the past.

"I was almost a psychotic 'worrier,'" a business man told me. "But no more. My affairs and my whole life have taken an almost incredible turn for the better since I have learned to commit them to Him with perfect trust."

"Fear," a woman remarked to me, "is hell on earth. For years I was afraid of life. Finally, in my effort to escape it, I became an alcoholic. Two years ago I was instantly healed by the power of God. I am free at last. I have put my hand in His, and I can never be afraid again."

There are very few of us who will not find ourselves recipients of the fringe benefits of the Christian faith—health and joy—if we follow the simple prescription consisting of two ingredients: daily devotions and, if possible, weekly attendance at a healing service. For the Church, which is the Body of Christ and the extension of the Incarnation, is as indispensable as your private devotions.

Christianity is a communal affair. It is not the individual worshiping God alone, in his own way, although it is that, too. It is also joining in corporate worship; the refilling of your spiritual cup from the continuous spring of Christ's power so uniquely present in the Church. At a healing service you will be spiritually irradiated; exquisitely aware of the Presence who extends a personal and perpetual invitation: "Come unto me . . . and I will refresh you."

Bringing comfort to the comfortless, hope to the despairing, and the living Christ to all who seek Him, the healing Church is the shrine which welcomes, in His Name, the sick and the fearful, the sinful and the sorrowing, the weak and the spiritually hungry. You will find its altar the point of contact which electrifies and recharges your entire being, flooding your life with the incandescence of the Holy Spirit.

CHAPTER 8

A Healing Ministry
in Every Church

℃HROUGH the healing ministry I have seen those starving for the Bread of Life fed. Their hunger has been forever assuaged by the demonstrable evidence of the living God.

The scores of clergy with whom I have talked are in unanimous agreement that the healing ministry is the most dynamic and thrilling phase of their work. Many have confessed that it was in their administration of spiritual healing that they felt for the first time the undeniable Presence of Christ. Why, then, has not every church a healing ministry?

After talking to many ministers who are interested in healing, but have not yet begun services, I believe that their reluctance to enter the healing field personally is due more frequently to a misunderstanding of spiritual healing than to disagreement with its theological premise. I have noted that when the clergy more fully understand the healing ministry and that when they observe first-hand the administration of spiritual healing and its results, more and more institute healing services.

Faith healing not spiritual healing

Typical of these clergymen is one who a year ago objected that in spiritual healing too much emphasis is placed on physical healing. His protest is a common one, due to a prevalent misconception of spiritual healing. He was confusing it with faith healing, which, although the terms are often used synonymously, is not at all the same thing. The latter, accurately speaking, does not necessarily have anything to do with Christian healing. It need not be, and indeed it frequently is not God-based.

Dr. Alexis Carrel has noted that "extreme acceleration of the processes of organic repair can effect so-called miracles of healing." This acceleration can be caused by faith in anything —a healer, a doctor, a bottle of tonic. When a physical cure appears to result from this type of belief, the spirit is left untouched and unhealed. When cure comes as a result of prayer through the clergy who serve as channels for the healing power, and is accompanied by spiritual regeneration, it becomes the spiritual healing practiced by the Church.

The ministry of healing, with its roots in the Incarnate Christ, is above all a spiritual ministry. The term "spiritual healing" means far more than physical healing achieved by spiritual methods. It means a healing of the whole nature of man by the power and grace of Our Lord. When the soul and the spirit are healed, so usually is the body. Those who have been so healed have known the presence of the Lord in a special and wonderful way. Surely no clergyman who understands this can object. There can be no over-emphasis on the healing of sick souls and ailing spirits, for such has been the mission of the Church since the time of Christ.

When the clergyman I mentioned thoroughly understood the intent of the healing ministry, he instituted healing services. A few weeks ago he said to me: "I have learned that spiritual healing is a very, very spiritual ministry. If not one physical cure had resulted, which fortunately is not the case, I would institute a healing ministry wherever I was because of the extraordinary spiritual blessings it imparts, both to the minister and laymen."

Church support for healing ministries

Because healing is at once the newest as well as the oldest of the Church's ministries, it is necessarily the most immature. Handling the power of God is not a responsibility which can be lightly undertaken. We should be aware that the healing ministry is fraught with danger, as is every aspect of religion; but as we do not eschew the Christian faith because of its fanatics, neither should we shun spiritual healing because we fear its inevitable lunatic fringe. We must remain alert to the threat that the body's health may be over-emphasized to the exclusion of the spiritual, which could result in the perversion of the healing ministry into heresy. But the potential hazards inherent in spiritual healing constitute the most valid reason—the extreme necessity—for keeping the healing ministry within the Church where it belongs; where the theological aspects of health and wholeness may be continually impressed.

The New Testament preaches a Gospel of physical as well as spiritual redemption (*Romans 8:23*). To keep that Gospel in its proper proportion, it should be preached in the organized Church. If it is not, people will go where it *is* preached, and too often over-emphasized.

Jesus mediated His healing power to the Church. By fulfilling His commission in its totality—"Preach ye the Kingdom and heal the sick"—and by correlating the healing ministry into the total life of the Church, spiritual healing can be protected from distortion.

As the promulgator of the Christian faith and the fountainhead of the Holy Spirit, it is the Church which must safeguard the healing Power from degeneration into chicanery, and the operation of the Holy Spirit from prostitution into either psychic or "faith" healing. It is the Church which must serve as the perpetual reminder that it is the soul's conversion which is the greatest of all miracles, the one to be most avidly sought and the goal of true spiritual healing.

Vocation unnecessary for healing ministry

Two years ago I talked with a clergyman who voiced a misapprehension shared by many of his fellow theologians. "I firmly believe in spiritual healing," he said, "but I have no healing gift, no vocation."

No minister refuses to preach because he has no "vocation" for speaking. He does not refuse to counsel because he has no "vocation" for guidance. He does not refuse to organize fellowship groups because he has no "vocation" for organization. All these activities are part of his entire vocation to the Church's ministry. So is spiritual healing. No minister needs a special healing vocation, for every ordained man, by virtue of his ordination, has the power and authority to heal in the Name of Jesus Christ.

I saw this same clergyman a short while ago. He told me that soon after our first talk a woman came to him and asked to be anointed for healing. "I told her frankly that I knew nothing of the service, and had never seen Unction administered. She was so persistent that I finally told her that if she would bring me a copy of the service the following week, I would borrow some consecrated oil."

The woman procured a manual from the Order of St. Luke, and received Holy Unction on the appointed day. She was instantly healed. "At that moment," the minister commented,

"I knew exactly what St. Peter meant when he said: 'Ye men of Israel, why marvel ye at this? . . . as though by our own power or holiness we had made this man to walk?'" (*Acts 3:12*).

Healing is only one of the ministries of the Church, but it is a vital one upon which the fruitfulness of the entire ministry seems to depend. More and more of the clergy are recognizing that, if the Christian faith is to be imparted in its entirety, healing must be restored as a normal part of every ministry.

The Reverend Albert Baller, a Congregationalist pastor trained in psychotherapy, speaks for many of today's clergy when he says: "My recently acquired knowledge of spiritual healing has caused me to do some careful revising of my thinking about the purpose of the Church and where the pastor's greater efforts should be placed. I am quite certain that we will be led, in the not too distant future, to make the spiritual healing services an important part of every church's total program."

Spiritual healing and counseling

Some ministers are concerned over what they believe to be the time-consuming element of the healing ministry. "I'm so busy already," said one, "that I simply can't undertake the extensive counseling I understand is necessary for spiritual healing."

Some healing churches emphasize counseling more than others, but many ministers have come to believe that in the effort to prepare patients for spiritual healing, the counseling aspect of this work has been over-emphasized. The Reverend John Maillard, Anglican priest highly instrumental in the recovery of the healing ministry in England, states that no more and no less counseling is required for spiritual healing than for Holy Communion.

There is no indication that Jesus used the psychiatric approach in His healing ministry; likewise, many today who seem impervious to medical treatment are healed by the di-

rect intervention of the Holy Spirit without benefit of counseling—healed not only of physical disabilities, but of mental
and nervous disorders as well.

A homosexual, for example, who was unsuccessfully treated
by psychiatry over a period of years, finally consulted his pastor. After two brief sessions, in which were explained the
purifying, healing power of God's love, the patient began attending healing services. Within a few weeks he was completely well, and is now happily married.

Or take the scores of instantaneous and complete healings
of alcoholism, which are taking place under the ministry of
healing. Many of these cases have spent thousands of dollars
on unavailing psychiatric care and futile hospitalization. Suddenly they respond to His healing touch. As one said: "I hadn't
been inside a church for years. At my wife's pleading I went,
with tongue in cheek, and received the laying-on-of-hands.
Then and there I felt the real Presence of Christ, and at that
precise moment I lost all desire for alcohol. That was five
years ago. I haven't had a drink since, and what is even more
wonderful, I haven't even wanted one!"

The clergyman, it should be understood, is a physician of
souls, not of minds and bodies. He should no more be expected to psychoanalyze than to perform surgery. It is interesting that those with the largest and most notable healing
ministries are forced to limit strictly the time they devote to
counseling. St. Paul said: "I determined not to know anything among you, save Jesus Christ, and Him crucified" (*I
Corinthians 2:2*). This often proves to be all that is necessary
to know today for healing.

Christ's power to heal unchanged

A Methodist minister states that he was taught in seminary,
and had for years unquestioningly believed that "miracles"
were confined to the New Testament. "But in view of what I
see happening," he says, "I am convinced that Christ is heal-

ing as surely today as He did during His earthly ministry."

There are many people, clergymen and laymen alike, who still honestly believe that Christ's healing ministry was not meant to continue into our time. It seems to me, however, that if this contention is followed to its logical conclusion, it must result in two things: first, a categorical denial of the historicity of the early Church, which was a healing church; and, second, a violation of what I understand to be a basic Christian tenet: the immutability of Jesus Christ, who is the same yesterday, today, and forever. If He is not the same today as He was yesterday, then He has changed—and change must be for the better or worse. Either Jesus was not perfect and has changed for the better; or He was perfect, and has changed for the worse. In either case, He could not be the perfect Son of God upon which our religion has been predicated.

"It was only recently that I realized this," remarked a young Presbyterian minister. "If His command to preach the kingdom and heal the sick was valid two thousand years ago, it must be equally valid today. If He has retained the power to save souls, it is hardly likely that He would have lost the lesser power to heal bodies."

Concerning the theological aspects of the healing ministry, the Reverend Richard Winkler of Chicago comments: "If a minister thinks spiritual healing theologically "wrong," let him step into a church where there is an active healing ministry and observe the saved souls and healed bodies that come about as a result. The practical effects are far more convincing than any theological arguments which may be expounded."

No failures in spiritual healing

Probably the most prevalent deterrent to the institution of healing services continues to be the fear of failure. Again and again the question is asked: "But what happens to a person's faith if he is not healed? Won't he then turn completely from God?"

The answer is an unequivocal "No," as anyone with a healing ministry will testify. But this is something which can only be learned, and believed, after personal experience.

The Reverend Don Gross, who has had extensive experience in the healing field, speaks for the healing clergy, when he says: "We pray, expectantly and with the conviction that God intends health. Sometimes the people we pray for die, or the disease remains; but people who have undertaken prayer for spiritual healing do not become discouraged or rebellious. Knowing His yearning to bestow life and health, their love for God abundantly increases, and their faith is invariably strengthened through their prayers for healing."

Those who have earnestly sought spiritual healing are never left unhealed. If the body is not healed, the spirit is.

Take the case of a young nurse who discovered that she had an inoperable cancer. She attended a number of healing services, with no discernible physical improvement; but her serenity and obvious happiness were an inspiration to those who knew her. When weakness and pain finally forced her to bed, her minister administered Holy Unction twice a week. After the second week, her pain left; and, to the amazement of her doctors, she was able to discontinue the use of morphine.

The day she died, three months later, she said to her minister: "Neither God nor His Church has failed. I have had a revelation of His Kingdom. I know now that this is only the beginning of a fuller life."

Joyfully and confidently she went into the outstretched arms of Christ, having been blessed by a gift from God not often given to those on earth. His power had transformed her faith into knowledge, her hope into certitude.

Not only are there no "failures" in true spiritual healing, but many of the clergy consider it the most universally successful of all their ministries. As an Episcopalian priest comments: "When I think of the word failure in regard to my work, I never couple it with spiritual healing. I think of Baptism, for the country is filled with baptized pagans; or I think of Confirmation, for my parish is filled with lapsed communicants. But in spiritual healing, spiritual grace is *always* received. Where physical healing does not result, it is received to an extraordinary degree."

Experience indicates that there appears to be no basis for the fear on the part of those unfamiliar with the healing ministry that a patient who does not receive physical healing will be psychologically harmed; will tend to blame himself, or doubt the sincerity of his own faith. He realizes that as so-called failures to heal are not the fault of God, neither are they necessarily his. He knows that an unhealed body is no more the will of God than a sinful world, and that both are the result of human weakness, of corporate faithlessness, and mass disobedience. The gloom of centuries of unbelief cannot be instantly and universally dispelled; the thunder of man's doubt and misunderstanding cannot be immediately and wholly silenced.

Total health is the will of God

Nevertheless, the healing clergy, convinced that total health is the primary will of God and believing that Jesus is the Saviour of our bodies as well as our souls (*Ephesians* 5:23), are not relaxing their efforts to determine the cause of the physical failures of spiritual healing. Meanwhile they emphasize that while some unknown, alien factor may have hindered the healing of the body, nothing can impede God's healing of the spirit. Experience testifies to the magnificent truth, that none who turn to Him remain unhealed.

Never have I seen this more convincingly demonstrated than in an Episcopal Church where I happened to be speaking a few months ago.

After the service a pale, obviously ill man came up to me

to tell me of his illness from which the doctors had given him one chance in a million of recovering.

"I have attended healing services for two months," he said, "and I've grown continually worse. What can I do?" Without waiting for an answer, he asked the question uppermost in the minds of all who are very ill. "Have you ever heard of a case like mine being healed?"

To know that someone has been healed of the same ailment from which we suffer is, understandably, a tremendous faith-booster. Happily I could give him an affirmative answer, as has been the case whenever this question is asked, for I believe that every disease known to modern man has responded to the healing power of God.

As I detailed the healing of a case similar to his, I saw the despair in his eyes replaced by hope. I observed that what appeared to be a purely intellectual assent that God could and would heal seemed now to tremble on the brink of emotional acceptance of that fact.

The result was that, after asking to make a sacramental confession, the first in his life, the patient was anointed at ten-thirty that night at the altar of a church filled with the power of the Holy Spirit. A spiritually transformed man walked down the altar steps at the conclusion of the service. The expression in his eyes, the indefinable but unmistakable radiance about him must have been remarked by even the most skeptical. To the believers there seemed no doubt that he had been touched by the healing Hand of Christ.

"I've never felt such peace and joy," he said. "It doesn't matter now whether my body is healed or not. I've found something better than physical health."

When I left the city that night I had no idea whether or not his disease had been cured, but I knew that he had been marvelously healed. I have learned since that this man has completely recovered his health.

Only a few years ago, a religious healing was a rare occurrence. Today the statistics offered by the Reverend Alex

Holmes, English Congregationalist, are, as nearly as I can ascertain, typical. This great young leader of the healing ministry in the Free Churches in Britain, states that forty per cent seeking help under his ministry, are completely healed, forty per cent greatly benefited, and the remaining twenty per cent, although not physically helped, are spiritually aided to an outstanding degree.

God lives in the healing ministry

As the healing ministry expands, and the faith of the whole Church quickens; as the discordant voices of doubt diminish, and more and more Christians turn to Our Lord, daring to claim His promise that all who ask in His Name shall receive (*John 14:13*), we see that complete healings are occurring in ever-increasing number. Those long deaf now hear His voice with unprecedented clarity; and those long blind perceive with new insight the meaning of His words: "He that believeth on me, the works that I do shall he do also; and greater works than these shall he do" (*John 14:12*).

All men everywhere have longed for the definite assurance, the concrete evidence that God lives. We have it now in the healing ministry which has made the good news of the Gospel a reality.

We are fully aware that "blessed are those who have not seen and yet have believed." But we remember, too, that Our Lord did not withhold from His doubting disciple the proof of His identity. "Reach hither thy hand, and thrust it into my side," He said to Thomas, "and be not faithless, but believing" (*John 20:27*).

And so, today, a merciful God has had compassion on us of little faith. He again offers us the evidence of His mighty acts, "that ye might believe that Jesus is the Christ, the Son of God; and that believing ye might have life through His name" (*John 20:31*).

Through this evidence I have seen countless unbelievers

brought to God. I have seen the passive belief of thousands of nominal Christians blaze into flaming faith. Wherever the healing ministry is in effect, I have seen the spiritual life of the community immeasurably strengthened; the spiritual power of the Church inestimably enhanced.

Because of these things, it seems to me that it is the holy obligation of the Church, and the sacred duty of the believing laity, to create a universal awareness of the healing Christ —an awareness before which a troubled, searching world must fall to its knees, echoing the words of Thomas, "My Lord and My God."

CHAPTER 9

"When Two or Three Are Gathered Together"

Our Lord promised us that, when two or three are gathered together in His Name, He will grant their requests.

Thousands of prayer groups, not only in the United States but all over the world, are claiming this promise with magnificent results. These groups are part of the growing laymen's movement to strengthen the Church's ministry. They are translating the Sunday Gospel into a meaningful seven-day-a-week way of life.

Roberta Fletcher, a pioneer in the healing field, and one of the most outstanding and inspired leaders in healing prayer group work, says: "The corporate prayer work of laymen is a God-given commission as certainly as the healing ministry is the privilege and responsibility of the clergymen of our churches."

Laymen today are striving to fulfil this commission. The

fruitful results of their efforts have done much to hasten the restoration of the Church's healing ministry.

All prayer has power. As a world-famous surgeon has commented: "It could not happen that any man or woman could pray for a single moment without some good result." Yet it is through corporate prayer, when minds and hearts are united in unselfish love and complete faith, praying in His Name with a single, common purpose, that we realize so frequently the unlimited power of God.

The protective power of prayer

That prayer is an actual, palpable force will not be denied by any who have experienced its effects. Among the most dramatic demonstrations of the protective power of prayer are the wartime experiences of so many men. Instance after instance is recorded of those saved by prayer from situations of desperate danger. An Englishman reports that every man in his regiment carried with him at all times a printed copy of the Ninety-first Psalm, which he prayed as continuously as possible. Not one man was lost from that regiment in four years of combat. In view of what we now know about the actual power of prayer, it no longer seems purely coincidental that so many parishes with active prayer groups report that they lost not a single boy during the Korean War.

My first personal experience with prayer as an almost physically discernible power came not during danger and not during illness, but during my first speaking tour on the subject of spiritual healing. I was nervous about talking on a subject which was still comparatively new to me and wholly foreign to all my previous training and experience.

As I stood for my first address, looking apprehensively over the large and well-filled church, I suddenly and distinctly felt what can best be described as a wall of protection completely surrounding me. So actual and concrete a thing did it seem that I had the impression that if I reached out my hand, I could touch it. My nervousness was immediately and wholly dissipated—and I proceeded with my talk.

Later that evening I mentioned this experience to a member of the church. "Yes," she said, "That's understandable. You see our prayer group joined together in prayer for you as you stood to speak. We have made arrangements with other groups so that you will be prayed for twenty-four hours a day as long as you are in our State."

I felt the impact of those prayers throughout my visit. Time after time since then I have experienced the same phenomenon, as have many others. This cannot be written off as "imagination" or "wishful thinking." The conviction frequently occurs, as it did in my case, when the subject knows nothing of the prayers being offered in his behalf.

Take another typical example. At six o'clock one evening not long ago, a friend telephoned to tell me, hysterically, that she had just received a medical verdict from her doctor: cancer of the uterus.

Immediately I called the leader of a prayer group, and asked that as many members as possible be requested to pray for my friend at 7:30 that same evening. I stopped by the patient's home about nine P.M. ostensibly to cheer her up, and found her confident and serene—a far cry from the hysterical woman to whom I had spoken a few hours before.

"The strangest thing happened," she said. "I was so upset and frightened I just went all to pieces. Right in the middle of drying the dinner dishes I suddenly felt a sense of complete security and peace come over me. I don't know how to express it, but I felt a physical sense of protection, as if I were inside some sort of protective barrier."

Dr. Alexis Carrel saw a cancer shrivel to a scar before his eyes while he was at Lourdes. He knew then that the physical results of prayer were neither imaginary nor coincidental. "Prayer," he was later to say, "is the most powerful form of energy that can be generated. It is a force as real as terrestrial

gravity. It is the only power in the world that seems to overcome the so-called 'laws of nature.'"

An increasing number of his colleagues are beginning to
agree with him; for so often does either a complete healing
or dramatic improvement take place either at the exact time
of prayer or immediately afterward, that the results of prayer
are no longer universally dismissed as accidental.

Take the case of a patient suffering severe pain from a
ruptured disc. A prayer group prayed for this patient at 7:30
one evening. At 8:30 he reported that he was suddenly free
from pain. The scheduled surgery was subsequently canceled,
and over a period of more than three years he has remained
symptom free.

Or take the case of a man whose one remaining kidney had
ceased to function. After he was rushed to the hospital, his
wife was told that he was dying from uremia. She immediately
telephoned her minister, who promptly called a special prayer
meeting. From that hour on the patient began to improve.
His recovery was rapid and complete. "Miraculous" was his
physician's comment.

Medical cooperation with prayer groups

Not only are doctors beginning to ascribe the healing of
medically hopeless cases to a Higher Power, but some of
them are actively cooperating with prayer groups by joining
such groups themselves and by enlisting their aid in the treatment of patients.

One such doctor tells of a four-year-old child brought to him
for treatment. The little boy had never taken a step in his
life and was blind, deaf, and dumb. The physician called the
leader of a local prayer group and requested prayers for the
wholeness of the child. A few weeks later the small boy was
brought back to his office. He walked in, went to the window,
pulled open the blind, and laughed aloud. This is the power
of God released by prayer.

Some doctors regularly call in local prayer groups in the case of critically ill patients. I saw this type of cooperation in action not long ago.

While I was discussing prayer with a group leader in Texas, her telephone rang. It was a doctor from a local hospital asking that she and three other members of the prayer group report as quickly as possible to the hospital to pray for a critically injured accident victim who had just been brought to Emergency. Within ten minutes she had contacted the other members of the group. In less than an hour they were at the hospital, kneeling in prayer at the patient's bed while a clergyman laid on hands.

Group prayer is in the great tradition of the Christian Church, instituted by Our Lord on the night of the Last Supper when He led His disciples in prayer (*John: 17*), and carried on by the apostles and their converts as they met in secret upper rooms. "When two or three are gathered together, there am I in the midst" has become today, as it was in the early Christian Church, a demonstrable truth.

Healing prayer circles are considered by clergymen to comprise a vital and indispensable part of their healing ministries. "Were this ministry not supported and strengthened by the believing prayers of our group," says the pastor of one church, "I would not have undertaken it." Many ministers attribute the effective results of their healing ministries to the fact that each service is attended by at least five members of the healing prayer group, all offering prayers for the sick.

Prayer groups a source of healing ministries

A number of clergymen consider the formation of a prayer group the initial step toward the institution of healing services in the church. In more than one instance (and this should be of interest to any layman who would like to see the healing ministry revived in his church) it has been the tremendously effective work of a group of dedicated, praying laymen which has induced a formerly hesitant minister to institute healing services in his church.

An outstanding example of this is found in North Miami, Florida, where the work of the prayer group organized and led by Mrs. Adele Miller resulted in a revival of the healing ministry, not only in her own church, the Church of the Resurrection, but also in several other churches in the vicinity.

Four years ago Mrs. Miller was seriously ill physically, mentally, and spiritually. After her name was placed by a relative on the prayer list of St. Stephen's Church in Philadelphia, she found her health improving. Through reading literature on spiritual healing, and through the help of her rector, Father Charles James, and the Reverend Ben Schumacher, she completely recovered her health. Anxious to pass on her new knowledge of the healing Christ, she formed a prayer group of interested women, beginning with only five members.

One of their first prayer results was the healing of a man desperately ill of tuberculosis. This was followed by the healing of a chronically sick woman, who learned through prayer group work to forget herself and pray for others.

This small prayer group, which now forms the local branch of the Order of St. Luke, then went to Father James and requested that he institute healing services. Observing the work and methods of the group, he readily acquiesced. Each weekly Communion service at the Church of the Resurrection is now immediately followed by the laying-on-of-hands.

As the laymen's movement grows, more and more prayer groups are being formed. Many are interdenominational. Working harmoniously together in love, unity, and understanding, the members are demonstrating for all to see the power of the healing Christ which is the heritage of all Christians, regardless of church affiliation. They have accepted their responsibility as Christians to be "Disciples of His Words." They have recognized that salvation of one's own soul is not the only obligation of the Christian; and that it is very often in our attempts to save others that we ourselves are saved. Like the disciples gathered with one accord in one place, the "fellowship of the concerned" is witnessing to the power of the risen Lord in human life.

Prayer transcends distance

As there is no limit to the power and love of God, so is there no spatial limit to the power of intercessory prayer. People in Europe have felt the beneficence of prayers offered by groups in California. Nor is the influence exerted by interdenominational prayer circles confined to the curing of sick souls and ailing bodies. Their example of concord, unselfish love, and a unity of faith in the healing Christ is doing much to bridge the chasm which divides various denominations.

The often far-reaching results of group prayer is typified by an instance which occurred several years ago.

A young girl suffering from a brain tumor was prayed for simultaneously by several groups, including one in Lincoln, Nebraska and one in Dallas, Texas, shortly before she went into the operating room. When her skull was incised, the surgeon was flabbergasted to find no evidence of the tumor which had been so clearly visible in the X-rays. Her recovery was complete and permanent. But this healing did not end with the patient. An entire community was made thrillingly aware of the healing Christ. Prayer groups were started in the locality where the patient's family lived, and a longstanding schism between two churches was healed.

Prayer is the means of unleashing the greatest force on earth. It is the means of releasing God's power into our lives and affairs. If every one of us were to live perpetually surrounded by the prayers of others, neither sin nor sickness could penetrate that protective armor.

If prayer were more widely understood and generally practiced, it would recreate the world, for the power of God for good can destroy all evil. Helen Shoemaker, who is one of the country's great leaders in the general prayer group movement, says: "It is my conviction that the people of prayer hold the real balance of power in the world. It is only when we begin to pray as Christ taught us to do that we can hope to lift the dark cloud of evil hanging so heavily over the heads of us all."

Jesus assured His apostles that "Ye shall receive power, after that the Holy Ghost is come upon you" (*Acts 1:8*). As we grow in spiritual understanding, we find that this power is equally available to us. It is being thrillingly demonstrated by those small bands of people who meet together in prayer, striving to fulfil His words.

CHAPTER 10

How to Start

a Prayer Group

$\mathcal{9}$ F YOU would like to start a prayer group and are not quite sure how to go about it, the experience of others may be helpful.

The logical place to begin is within your own church, where you are apt to find like-minded people, and where your minister will be able to help you.

A typical group got its start in Pittsburgh three years ago when a young man and his wife discussed the matter with their clergyman and procured from him the names of several other couples who he thought might be interested. They subsequently invited four couples to their home one evening, and from this meeting evolved a group of eight people who were eager to grow together in spiritual experience. Weekly meetings were established, and within a year the group had expanded to the point where it was necessary to subdivide it into three separate circles.

From the original group there also evolved a neighborhood women's group which meets one morning a week. This prayer fellowship continues to expand, and one of its original members, Mrs. Patricia Naugle, comments: "We all find our lives tremendously enriched spiritually. Learning more of how to pray and discovering something of how the Holy Spirit works in our lives has enabled us to find answered prayer in the form of problems solved, needs met, and physical and spiritual healings. We know a peace and joy not of this world."

If your minister is unable to help you in your prayer group efforts, contact a few people on your own. Ask them to your house and talk the matter over with them. Don't let lack of numbers deter you, for many prayer fellowships have begun with only two or three members meeting for study, discussion, and prayer.

An extremely effective group was started in Dallas, Texas, a few years ago by Mrs. Lella Whiteman. She reports that in the beginning there were many weeks when only she and her husband attended the scheduled "meetings." But they persevered, and gradually the group expanded. Known now as the Upper Room Prayer Group, this circle is an impressive witness to the power of prayer, as was demonstrated in the healing of an acute alcoholic. The patient underwent surgery and was found to be suffering from advanced cirrhosis of the liver. The surgeon estimated that he would not live over thirty days, and these under the influence of strong narcotics to alleviate the intense pain. A relative asked prayers for the critically ill man. The patient went into a deep sleep that same afternoon and awoke free from pain. From that time on no narcotics were necessary, as there was no recurrence of pain. He was, at the same time, instantly healed of alcoholism—and today, years later, he is medically certified a well man in every respect.

Starting a prayer group

Prayer group studies have resulted in the conclusion that the ideal size for a prayer circle is not fewer than six or more than fourteen persons. Nevertheless, don't be discouraged or fail to meet because your group may still be limited in size to three or four members. There is a new group which meets in an Episcopal Church once a week directly before the healing service begins. On numerous occasions only three of the group has turned up. Yet this tiny circle has dramatically demonstrated the promised power when two or three are gathered together in His Name. More important than the number is that each member of the group is making a sincere effort to grow spiritually. The most effective prayer groups, regardless of size, are those whose members all engage in daily meditation and prayer.

When you have discussed your proposed healing prayer group with your clergyman, and have contacted a nucleus of individuals interested in the project, your next concern is where to meet, how often, and how to conduct the meetings when they are underway.

Some groups meet in the homes of members; some in churches; some in library rooms. Probably for a beginning circle, which is usually small, a private house is the best answer. How often you meet is up to your membership. Generally speaking, the most active and effective groups meet once a week, for it has been found difficult to establish and sustain the rapport between members, so vital to corporate prayer, with less frequent meetings.

Experience indicates that in order to assure unity and power in your group prayer, you must meet regularly, always planning your meetings in advance so that they will not be haphazard. The meetings should be limited to approximately one hour. Above all, the members of your group must be in love and fellowship with one another. If there is any anger, hostility, or resentment present, the prayer power will be non-existent.

Before your first scheduled meeting, appoint a leader. It can be either the host or hostess, if you are meeting in a home, or you can appoint a leader to serve by the month or whatever term is agreeable to your group.

Outline for prayer group meetings

The following outline for a meeting is used, with minor variations, by many groups. It can be adapted to suit the preference of any particular circle.

1. Have your group sit in a circle. If the group is sufficiently small, members can sit around a table.

2. The leader opens the meeting with a prayer, which can be either spontaneous or taken from the Book of Common Prayer or any other prayer manual. Spontaneous prayer is always to be encouraged, but don't force it in the beginning. Let the members grow into it.

3. A selected reading from Scripture.

4. A brief period of silent meditation. There is great power in united silence, but don't allow the silent period to persist too long, for the attention tends to wander. Close the meditation with a short prayer by the leader.

5. This is the time of "witness," obeying the injunction of Our Lord to "Go and tell." Let the members relate recent experiences of answered prayer, sharing with the others personal spiritual experiences.

6. Study period. This can consist of reading on the subject of spiritual healing, either one chapter from a book or a magazine article or pamphlet. The Order of St. Luke can supply you with material suitable for your group.

7. A short discussion period on what has been read. Here the leader should take a tactful but firm hand to prevent rambling irrelevancies.

8. Announcement of next meeting and lesson assignment, if any.

9.Intercession. This fifteen-minute period can be opened by the leader with a prayer of praise and thanksgiving. Then the first names of those on the prayer list (which was earlier submitted to the leader) will be read aloud, and prayers offered for them. These names may include any members of the group who are themselves in need of healing. Your intercession might well be concluded with prayers for the healing church and the whole world; with special prayers offered for any national or international problem current in the news. Many groups hold hands during this entire period of intercession.

10. The leader now closes the meeting with a prayer of general thanksgiving, ending with repetition of the Lord's Prayer.

Your prayer group is now ready to adjourn. Before going home, you may want to enjoy some social fellowship with your prayer circle, for as Mrs. Naugle points out, "Friendships made here, not with just a social background, but with true concern and love for one another, far transcend the ordinary sort."

Time will disclose the most feasible and effective way for your group to function. Your circle may decide to pray daily at home for those in need, at a stipulated time, so that your prayers will be offered in unison. Or, in addition to your weekly meetings, you may want to attend healing services as a group, praying for the sick. Or you may prefer to function more informally, appointing a telephone committee which will relay to other members the names of those desiring prayer —no specific time for prayer being set, except in cases of emergency.

When your group expands sufficiently, you may decide to function as does the Prayer Healing Fellowship at St. Stephen's Church in Philadephia—dividing into teams, each praying for a specific half hour, so that prayers are being offered almost around the clock.

Prayer lists

As time goes on, you will probably find your group confronted with various questions. How long, for example, should the same names be carried on a prayer list? Experience has proved that you will find it advisable to set a definite time limit. Some groups carry names for as long as a month, others for only a week, depending on the circumstances of the particular need.

The prayer chain affiliated with St. Peter's Episcopal Church, Brentwood, Pittsburgh, handles this matter in a fairly typical way. Here prayers are offered for those on the so-called "active" list, for a period of ten days. If continued prayer is requested, the group continues for another ten-day period.

A "permanent" list is also kept of those requiring prayer for a month or longer. This list is renewed at monthly intervals, if requested. This renewal process is necessary in order to keep in touch with those who are requesting prayer.

Then there is the question of how many names should be prayed for by one group. Some feel that the list should be limited in number. The Bishop of Coventry, England, for example, feels very strongly on this point. Practically, however, this seems virtually impossible to do; for no one can, in good conscience, refuse to pray when asked. It is interesting to note that Dr. Rettig and his Prayer Band pray for many hundreds, and a remarkable number of healings result. As Dr. Rettig comments: "To limit the number of people on our prayer list seems to me like limiting the power of God. We have to remember that it is God, not we, who heals—and His power is without confinement or 'limitation.'"

St. Stephen's, too, carries an enormously long prayer list. These names are as often prayed for as a group as individually.

We are all aware of the healing results of this fellowship.

However, if your group feels, as so many do, that more power is attached to prayer when personal concern and attention can be focused upon the particular individual in need of help, try to divide your list of names so that each member has only as many as he can handle.

Should a disease be named?

Whether to name the *disease* of the patient you are praying for is also a question which arises frequently. There is so wide a divergence of opinion on this point that it would seem advisable to discuss the matter with your group, and do whatever the majority decide upon.

There are those who feel that prayer concentrated on the specific ailment has greater power than a more generalized prayer for the "health" of the patient. Others feel that we are so conditioned to fear certain diseases such as cancer that negative thoughts may subconsciously intrude into our prayers. The possiblity of unwittingly and unconsciously enveloping a patient with fear is one that must be reckoned with. What you decide on this matter depends on your group. I have seen spectacular healings result from both methods of prayer.

Very much the same problem prevails in regard to prayer groups visiting and praying for patients medically termed "hopeless." Some, like the group I have previously mentioned, have achieved wonderfully effective results from this method. Others feel that they can pray more effectively for such patients if they do not see them. I can readily understand this attitude, as I remember so well my first experience with prayer for a so-called "hopeless" case.

I had been asked by the doctor in charge to go to the hospital and pray as a clergyman administered Holy Unction to a patient desperately sick with cancer. Now I had previously witnessed and verified many healings of so-called terminal cancers. I was completely confident of God's will and power to heal. Yet, when I walked into that hospital room and saw the unconscious patient, my heart sank. For a moment my faith faltered. It took every effort of which I was capable to envision that still figure on the bed as a completely whole and well man, which is so necessary a part of the healing technique.

Since that time I have found it considerably easier to eradicate any vision of illness, whether near or apart from the patient. I have learned to enter a sickroom, not with the disease on my mind, but rather with what God has to give that patient and anyone else who will receive in faith. Nevertheless, it is understandable how many prayer groups can function more effectively at a distance, just as some can function more effectively if they do not know the nature of the disease which afflicts those for whom they are praying.

If at all possible, find out what has happened to those you pray for. Some groups ask that this information be telephoned or written in. Others which function on a larger scale, such as the Society of the Nazarene, under the leadership of Mrs. Ethel Banks (who is magnificently carrying on her clergyman husband's work), send out cards at intervals, asking that they be returned, filled in with the pertinent information concerning the patient's progress, whether continued prayer is desired, etc.

Beware of pride in successful healings

For any healing or improvement reported to you, give thanks; but be constantly on guard that a feeling of pride does not develop. As Helen Reagan Smith, leader of an Oklahoma prayer group points out: "Let us begin to feel, 'We did that with *our* prayers,' and all power immediately evaporates from the group."

As we witness, with a wonder akin to awe, the power of the Risen Christ released in our lives by group prayer, we tend to overlook the fact that prayer of itself cannot heal. Rather does it serve as a window through which His light may shine. It is our longing for God, our humility in seeking Him, our earnest efforts to follow more closely in His footsteps, which enable that window to transmit His radiant energy.

The exact manner in which your fellowship elects to work is immaterial. All that matters is that each member is seeking a closer relationship with God; striving to release to others in need and to a sick world the healing power of Christ.

"Prayer," says Helen Shoemaker, "is the bridge that we throw across the space between our weakness and God's strength—a bridge over which He can walk into the lives of men and nations."

Every layman has a part in the construction of this bridge—a bridge conceived in faith, built on love, and dedicated to the living Christ. Your prayer group is one of its girders.

The candles lit by small groups of praying laymen will gradually expand the circle of His light until it illumines every corner of the earth. All darkness will then be dissipated. His Light will suffuse the world.

CHAPTER 11

The Power of Prayer:
The Story of Robert Byers

𝒩 OT LONG AGO a desperately ill boy made a remarkable recovery. The young man's family and friends and many inhabitants of the New England village where he had lived and gone to school believe that it was a miraculous healing. The consensus of medical opinion on the case is that regardless of the medical aid rendered the patient, without the healing power of God released by prayer, recovery would have been extremely unlikely. This is the story of that healing.

When Robert Byers, aged twenty-one, complained of fatigue on Thursday, July 11, 1957, his father, a lusty construction foreman, thought little of it. Young Bob, a junior at Grove City College, Pennsylvania, was not used to physical labor, and the construction work he had undertaken in Newfoundland as a summer job, was strenuous to say the least.

The following day, however, Bob was more than tired; he began to have trouble walking and moving his feet. Late that afternoon he was half-carried home from the job. The local doctor was unable to diagnose the trouble. Later that night, when Bob appeared to be growing paralyzed, a second doctor was called who proved equally bewildered. The next morning, completely unable to walk by now, the boy was taken to the Naval Dispensary, where, after a lengthy examination, he was ordered to remain overnight while further tests were conducted.

By noon Sunday his condition had drastically worsened. A consultation was held at the Dispensary, and a tentative diagnosis made: polyneuritis (Guillain Barre Syndrome), a sister disease to polio, with an adult death rate of two out of three.

As the Naval hospital lacked facilities to care for such a case, the doctors urged the patient's immediate return to the United States. Arrangements were quickly made by telephone for his admission to a Boston hospital. A Navy plane was ordered to be ready in two hours, equipped with oxygen and other emergency equipment. Meanwhile Bob's condition was growing progressively and rapidly worse, and it was necessary to perform a tracheotomy shortly before he boarded the plane.

At midnight on July 14 two doctors, the pilot and co-pilot, and Bob on a stretcher, accompanied by his parents, took off for the Boston airport. The Superintendent of the Naval Dispensary had telephoned Boston to have the custom and immigration men, as well as the ambulance on the field when the plane arrived.

For the first two hours after the Newfoundland take-off, the doctors worked frantically over Bob to keep him alive. Meanwhile his parents sat in their seats, frozen with fear. It was at this time that Monte Byers, the tough construction man whose sole claim to fame was that he could "swear louder and knew more curse words than anybody else" began to pray for, as he said, the first time in his life.

"Dear God, please hear the prayers of a sinner," he entreated. "Don't let Bob die. He's so young and so afraid, please give him a few more years. I don't even know how to pray, but please give me the knowledge."

A few minutes later the big, rugged pilot came back through the plane. He put his hand on the distraught father's shoulder. "We're praying, too," he said.

"This," said Mr. Byers, "rather startled me, because he didn't look any more like the type that prayed than I did. I wondered how he knew I was praying."

The plane was met by an ambulance with two attendants and two doctors. The family were quickly checked through customs and immigration, while Bob was transferred to the ambulance and rushed to the hospital.

By the time his parents arrived by taxi, the boy was ensconced in a private room outside of which were gathered thirteen doctors. In groups of four, they proceeded to enter the sickroom and examine the patient. At the end of an hour, the initial tentative diagnosis was confirmed: polyneuritis.

The doctor in charge explained to the Byerses that it was touch and go with Bob. His respiratory muscles were failing, and it was necessary to place him at once in an iron lung. The doctor went on to explain that the large group of doctors in attendance were house doctors who were being briefed on Bob's case so that in event of emergency all of them would know exactly what to do. Two of these doctors were assigned to sleep in the room next to the patient, with an oxygen therapist across the hall.

Within a few hours of his admission to the hospital, Bob was completely paralyzed from his feet to his eyes; even his eyelids could close only partially. His mental faculties and his power of speech were all that remained unimpaired.

Beds in the seldom-used hospital solarium were set up for the stunned parents. A vigil began which was to last for over four months.

"We lost all track of time," relates Mr. Byers, "even lost

track of the seasons. The days and nights seemed almost the same."

Friends began sending the Byers religious pamphlets. "One of our friends," says Mr. Byers, "was the librarian at Wickford, Rhode Island, who sent me a book called *A Reporter Finds God Through Spiritual Healing*. For awhile I was too nervous and upset to read it, but I kept handling it and carrying it from place to place, along with a pamphlet containing the Gospel of St. Luke. I tried not to let anyone see these for fear they'd think I had become a religious fanatic in desperation, or say, 'The old sinner is scared and now he wants God to help him.' That was exactly the case, but I didn't want them to know it.

"One day I started to read *A Reporter Finds God* and was impressed by the writer's own early reactions towards religion. Apparently they were the same as mine. The title said she had found God. I wanted to know how, and there wasn't much time. I knew I had to have His help before it was too late.

"I'd read a few paragraphs; then some emergency would occur in Bob's room. A lot of doctors would appear, go in and revive him, and then I'd try to read a little more. Finally as I read, I began to feel that if only I had enough faith, God would guide the doctors and Bob would get well. My prayer now became, 'Dear Father, give me more faith.'"

The Byerses now made it a habit to stop by the hospital chapel at least three times a day, on their way to the cafeteria for meals. They asked any friends or relatives who came to the hospital to join them in prayer. On a table in the solarium Mr. Byers kept a pamphlet always open to a Bible verse: "He giveth power to the faint; and to them that have no might He increaseth strength" (*Isaiah 40:29*).

"I kept reading this over and over hundreds of times," he said. "It seemed to describe Bob exactly, because he certainly was faint, and it promises that He increaseth strength. I'd read this and pray, and then go down to see if Bob looked any better."

The often-repeated and always heartbreaking plea of his son, "You won't let me die, will you, Dad?" echoed and re-echoed in the father's ears during the endlessly long, wakeful nights.

"When I couldn't stand it any longer," he recalls, "I'd go to the men's room where nobody could see me, and get on my knees on the floor and pray."

One Sunday morning in August it looked as if Bob could not last out the day. His sister and her husband were hastily summoned from Rhode Island, escorted to and from the airports by state police. At this time many different prayer groups in and around Wickford had been alerted to the situation. Both Protestants and Catholics met in churches and in homes to offer prayers for the boy they all knew.

By midafternoon on that Sunday Bob seemed less exhausted than in the morning, but another serious crisis developed; he had pneumonia. Fluid had developed in his lungs by the following day, and it became necessary to tap his side. During this operation his right lung collapsed, and two tubes were inserted in his chest, while air was pumped into an incision in his throat to enable him to breathe. Months later the chest surgeon on the case remarked: "The night I put those tubes in Bob's chest I never expected him to be alive the next morning."

But although he was alive, he was in critical condition. In the late afternoon he went into shock, and the doctors worked over him all night.

Relatives summoned from Pittsburgh and other members of the family gathered in the hospital. They spent most of the night praying in the solarium.

"We must have been a rather strange looking group gathered in that room," recalls Mr. Byers. "We would all get together and pray silently for a little while. Then, a few at a time, we would slip down to Bob's room and watch him. Then we would get together again, and someone would say, 'Let's have another prayer.'

"We were all scared. I can't describe how scared we were. We got the hospital chaplain to pray with us, but I had the distinct feeling that he didn't think Bob would pull through; that he was praying for *us* so that we wouldn't go to pieces when we lost him."

The next day the boy was in very poor condition. The doctors who had stayed with him twenty-four hours a day told his parents that they had done all they could, but that he was slipping fast.

"We felt so helpless," Mr. Byers said, "and we continued to question the doctors, longing for a ray of hope. When they couldn't give it to us, we'd say to them; 'All we can do, then, is pray.' To my surprise, every one of the many doctors on the case without exception replied in all sincerity: 'That will help.' "

By dint of transfusions and other emergency measures, Bob continued to hang on, barely alive, through August and September and into October. Much of this time his condition was so critical that six or eight members of the Byers family virtually lived at the hospital.

"As I look back now," remarked Mr. Byers, "I begin to realize how wonderful it was for this big institution to allow a family to practically move into it with a patient. We must have been pests to those busy doctors and nurses, always waylaying them and asking questions, but they were always courteous and kind, taking time to explain."

In the middle of October another blow struck. Bob's right lung had been severely damaged by the pneumonia and ensuing complications, and double surgery would be necessary. The first operation would involve the removal of one rib in order to insert a larger drainage tube; to be followed by a second in which the lower lobe of his lung would be removed. Only too well aware of their son's already extremely precarious condition, the boy's parents were terrified by the thought of this surgery. It was at this time, the week-end of October 19, that Mr. Byers called relatives in Glenshaw, Pennsylvania, asking them to contact Kathryn Kuhlman, the Pittsburgh evangelist mentioned in the book *A Reporter Finds God.*

"I wanted her to come to Boston," Mr. Byers said, "to conduct a healing service for Bob; and I wanted it made clear that, whatever the cost of the trip, I would pay for it."

Two days later Bob's cousin called from Pittsburgh. "Our minister has talked to Kathryn Kuhlman," he reported. "She says there's no need for her to go to Boston, for she can't heal anyone, only God can. And she can pray as well in Pittsburgh as she can in Boston. Now here's what she told us to do. Do you have a pencil? Write this down."

The boy was very excited as he relayed the message:

"This is important. Miss Kuhlman and her people here, and there are hundreds of them, will pray for Bob on Tuesday, Wednesday, and Thursday nights. On Friday at one o'clock, they will have a healing service for him. They will fast from Thursday midnight until Friday sundown, and she said all of you at Boston should also fast.

"Tell Bob all about it. She wants him to be aware of all that's going on. You are to keep praying as you have been, only here is the prayer everyone is to say: 'that God's power will work in Bob.' Don't pray for him to get well, just ask that God's power work in him.

"Tell Bob not be afraid, no matter how or what he feels. You and Aunt Adria are to be with him on Friday at one o'clock, and it is important that all of you keep repeating this prayer. Uncle Monte, be sure to tell Bob about my calling. We've both always been kind of skeptical about things like this, but tell him I said this is the greatest thing I have ever heard—that this is *real.*"

The boy's excitement and conviction were contagious. Mr. Byers' hopes rose. He read to his wife the instructions he had written down, and later to Bob. After he left the room Bob asked his mother: "Why is Dad doing all this? Can't the doctors do any more for me?"

She replied: "It isn't that, Bob. Your Dad is just trying to get you well."

They followed Miss Kuhlman's instructions. On Thursday night, so strong was their faith that they had their son's clothes pressed and shoes shined in the event that he would be able to leave the hospital after the Pittsburgh healing service.

At one o'clock on Friday, October 25, a number of the Byers' family and friends, all of whom were fasting, knelt in the Church at Wickford, saying the prayer. Mr. and Mrs. Byers were in Bob's room repeating it with him. A few minutes later in the middle of the prayer, Bob suddenly fell asleep. Curiously enough, his parents almost immediately followed suit. It was two weeks later that Bob's sister reported that she, too, had suddenly fallen asleep in the Wickford Church, sixty miles from Boston. "That sleep," they agreed, "seemed almost a supernatural thing. We all felt strangely peaceful and rested when we woke up."

When Bob awakened, still repeating the prayer, he said in disappointment to his father, "Nothing happened, Dad." To which his father replied: "Don't be discouraged, son; we don't know. God works in mysterious ways."

Three days later another X-ray of Bob's chest was made. The Byerses were told that the removal of his rib was not going to be necessary. In view of a clearly discernible change there now seemed a possibility that he might not have to undergo lung surgery of any kind.

The next day Bob, who had until now been fed entirely by tube, remarked that he was starved and asked for food. After disposing of the orange juice and cereal brought him, he promptly said, "What's for dinner?" When told the hospital was serving roast beef, he demanded some. The doctors at first adamantly refused, but at his insistence they finally gave permission. A roast beef dinner was served him that evening, and he ate every morsel.

X-rays continued to be taken at intervals. Each report was better. His lung healed completely, and he improved daily.

In a short time he could be taken off the respirator for an hour at a time. One night he turned off the machine himself for eight hours. The doctors were horrified, but he apparently suffered no ill effects. He was warned, however, to take it slowly. Gradually his time out of the machine increased until by the end of October he was out more than half the time. In early November the respirator was no longer needed. Meanwhile, as his father expresses it, "The paralysis had just rolled off him like rolling back a rug; first his face, then his arms and chest and legs."

On November 3, he was allowed to sit up and dangle his legs over the side of the bed for five minutes. On November 7, after four months of total paralysis, unable to move even a finger, he rolled himself out to the solarium in a wheel chair. A short while later Bob went home.

Today he is well, able to walk and drive a car. The only reminder of his illness is the physical therapy he is still undergoing to strengthen his long-unused muscles. When one of his doctors saw him a short while ago, tears ran down the man's face. "I never would have believed this possible," he said.

To Bob and his parents, the promise of St. James is an unquestionable reality. "Is any sick among you? Let him call for the elders of the church; and let them pray over him. . . . And the prayer of faith shall save the sick" (*James 5:14–15*).

"To us," says Mr. Byers, "Kathryn Kuhlman and her people were the elders of the church. Through her and the others all over the country who were praying with her, Bob got well. She must be a wonderful person. In June we're all going to Pittsburgh to thank her and her people personally for their prayers."

As is so frequently the case in spiritual healing, the story of Bob Byers has not ended with his own cure. Because of this evidence of answered prayer, because of this visible demonstration of the power and mercy of God, the spiritual perception of the Byers family and close friends, and of hundreds of others has been quickened and deepened. These people have been converted to the healing Christ.

For some a new and exciting awareness of His presence has replaced the former prosaic acceptance of a remote God; for others, a lip-service religion has been galvanized into a flaming faith; for many, prayer has now become a way of life.

Men and women who until Bob's sickness had really never prayed at all now kneel side by side each night. Prayers for the sick, spoken now with a new conviction that God's will is health, are already bearing fruit. Families whose Bibles have long lain gathering dust have opened them again and read aloud each day. In Wickford, many of the school children who prayed for their alumnus, Bob, and saw with their own eyes the answer to these prayers, will bear on their lives forever the imprint of a knowledge not to be found in textbooks.

"Bob is the living proof of a miracle performed by God," asserts his father. "It's just impossible to describe how your life changes when something wonderful like this happens. There is one thing I know: mine can never be the same again since Bob was healed and since I've learned that Christ is actually right here, ready to help anybody who turns to Him."

Many of those connected with this healing have expressed this same thought. In them is vividly apparent the peace, the joy, and the strong sense of security which inevitably accompany a regenerated faith.

Bob Byers and his family express their gratitude to Kathryn Kuhlman as an instrument of God's power, and to all who offered prayers. But many of those who prayed are even more grateful; for in Bob's healing they have felt for the first time the touch of God upon their own lives. Through fasting and prayer they, as surely as the boy who was healed, have come to know the living Christ.

CHAPTER 12

Medical Recognition
of the Healing Phenomenon

$\mathcal{I}$NCREASING scientific acknowledgment of the reality of spiritual healing has lifted that phenomenon from the realm of suspected crackpot-ism into that of impeccable respectability. The extent of the growth of the healing ministry can be measured by the amount of scientific curiosity it has aroused, and by the research it has engendered.

Just a few years ago, mere mention of "miraculous" healing evoked scathing derision from the medical profession. This situation is slowly but surely changing. While doctors are rightly cautious concerning alleged non-medical cures, an increasing number are beginning to agree with Dr. Howard Craven, of Washington, D.C., who said to me not long ago: "If we are to be honest, we have to face the truth that a large number of remarkable healings appear to be taking place without medical or surgical intervention. Many of these cannot be categorized as purely psychosomatic. Experience seems to justify the belief that spiritual healing completes the chain that welds the patient into an integrated, whole, happy, well, unit."

Five years ago the almost universal chant of doctors, when confronted with medically inexplicable healings, was "wrong diagnosis." Today many of these same men, now familiar with the healing phenomenon, believe that the continued affirmation that the medically-diagnosed disease never existed in the first place constitutes an unwarranted indictment against modern diagnostic methods and medical skill, and is neither an honest nor a realistic approach to the subject.

The Trinity of Body, Mind, and Spirit

Dr. Albert Reissner, Brooklyn psychoanalyst, expresses the new attitude toward illness held by many of his colleagues when he says: "More and more of us are becoming convinced of two things: first, that man is a trinity composed of body, mind, and spirit; and, second, that the underlying cause of most disease is spiritual. We have observed that unless a healing of the spirit takes place, the cure of the body or mind is not apt to be either complete or permanent."

This concept is perhaps not so scientifically revolutionary as it may appear at first glance; for actually the step is not long between the medically accepted fact that sick emotions breed sick bodies, and the dawning awareness of the relevance of the spirit to physical, mental, and emotional well-being.

In June, 1955, the American Medical Association held its annual convention at Atlantic City. The incoming president of the Association urged that his fellow-physicians "take more into the sickroom than your medical skill. . . . Unless we are willing to give of ourselves and our faith, our science will avail us little."

A recent article in the Journal of the American Medical Association, emphasizes that the old concept of the "godless" doctor is rapidly being stamped out. Medicine and religion are now working together more closely than in any other period of modern times. Studies to correlate more fully the body and the spirit are already under way—studies, interestingly enough, suggested and initiated by the medical profession.

It was at the request of numerous doctors affiliated with the Houston, Texas, Medical Center that a pioneering venture was undertaken not quite two years ago. Here an "Institute of Religion," under the auspices of five Protestant denominations, was established to function as an integral part of the medical center. The purpose was to foster a closer cooperation between clergymen and the medical profession, in order that "healing of the *whole* patient—body, mind, and spirit—may result. As one doctor puts it: "We believe that total health depends on healing the man who has the disease, not merely the disease the man has."

Here at Houston is the beginning of what promises to be a new era in the practice of both medicine and the Church. We find the clergy, functioning no longer as mere consolers, but as healers, working side by side with doctors, who are no longer only scientists, but practicing Christians as well.

Dr. Claude Forkner of Cornell University comments: "We do not know what it is that brings about recovery of a patient. I am sure, however, that often it is faith which is a most important factor."

The Faith of the Doctor

When a doctor, as well as his patient, has faith in the healing power of God, an astoundingly effective medical practice results. One of the nation's most eminent heart surgeons, who is associated with the Methodist Hospital in Houston, is a case in point.

This surgeon performs, with an extraordinary record of success, delicate and intricate heart operations on patients who come to him from every state in the Union. He conducts his work in an atmosphere permeated with faith. Himself a firm believer in God's healing power, he carefully screens each member of the four medical teams which work under his supervision. He accepts for duty only those doctors and nurses who avow their belief in God and in the power of prayer. The doctor, like his co-workers, never operates without first going to the hospital's interdenominational chapel to pray. He asks his nurses and his patients, who occupy some four floors in the hospital, to remain in prayer while he is in surgery. He is a highly skilled surgeon, but he reminds his patients that faith and prayer are vital factors in their complete recovery.

In talking to the wife of one of these patients I learned that her husband, who required an aorta transplantation to save his life, had been referred to this surgeon by their family physician, two thousand miles away.

"I was in a strange city," she said, "worried to death over my husband's precarious condition, but I shall always remember the heartwarming and inspiring experience of my association with that hospital. It was a marvelously strengthening thing to know that my husband was continuously surrounded by an atmosphere of almost palpable faith and prayer. The surgeon's highly successful record is not difficult to understand. I only wish there were more hospitals run along these lines."

There *are* other such hospitals. The Good Samaritan in Los Angeles is one, and there will soon be more. A symposium of physicians and clergymen in New York City has recently proposed that hospitals and medical schools inaugurate "departments of religion" in order to promote a better understanding of the spiritual needs of the sick. Just a few weeks ago a group of physicians from Johns Hopkins Hospital in Baltimore met in conference to determine the best and quickest means of establishing a religious center to function in connection with the hospital.

"We want our patients," said one of these doctors, "to be assured the maximum benefit which can be derived only from *total* healing treatment. We believe that cure of the body, if it does not take into account the spiritual aspect of every patient, comprises only a partial cure."

These physicians commented that they now refrained from using the word "terminal" in reference to any condition. Why? "We have seen too many so-called 'terminal' cases perfectly healed by the power of God" was the answer.

Psychiatry, too, has recognized the interdependence of science and religion in the complete healing of an individual. Where mental illness is concerned, a growing number of modern psychiatrists, in opposition to Freud, but in the footsteps of Jung, agree with Dr. Reissner that a vital factor in the patient's recovery is his return to religion. Concrete evidence of this change in thinking can be found in the recent opening of the Lutheran Medical Center in Brooklyn, New York. Operating under the direction of Drs. Paul Qualben and John Kildahl, this Center was founded and is staffed by trained psychiatrists who are also ordained ministers. These men are uniquely qualified to render both psychological aid and spiritual treatment to their patients.

When I first began my research on spiritual healing a few years ago and sought to procure medical confirmation of the alleged cures, I was met with uncompromising hostility by virtually every doctor I contacted. However, in traveling over the country during the past year, I have found the picture rather drastically changed. I have been asked by many doctors to go with them to the hospital to pray for critically ill patients. A no longer unique experience was one I had recently in the Southwest.

During an interview with a prominent physician on the staff of a large city hospital, he said to me: "No one knows better than I the power of God to heal. Time after time I have seen medically hopeless cases literally raised from the dead through prayer and the laying-on-of-hands. I consider the ministrations of the healing clergy just as vital to my patients' welfare as the medical treatment I can render them—

and I can assure you I do not stand alone in the medical profession in this conviction."

As I sat in the doctor's office, his telephone rang. He gave some rapid instructions, ending with, "I'll be at the hospital in ten minutes." Turning to me, he excused himself. "A patient is sinking. I have to leave at once."

On his way out he paused at his secretary's desk to ask her to contact a clergyman from a nearby church. "Ask him if he will meet me at the hospital as soon as possible to lay on hands."

The minister his secretary called was an Episcopalian with an outstanding healing ministry. The doctor was a Presbyterian, and the patient a Methodist.

Studies in the science of spiritual healing

During the past three years there have been held a number of seminars in Rye, New York, where, for the first time in history, doctors and psychologists, physicists and clergymen have met to discuss and attempt to fathom the now-acknowledged phenomenon of spiritual healing. A few of these doctors have gone on to Dr. J. B. Rhine's para-psychology staff in an endeavor to learn more of the phenomenon. Others are working with physicists on the theory that electric and magnetic fields are somehow involved. In this connection, a number of scientists are attempting to devise a method by which the "healing power" can be scientifically measured.

Under the auspices of the Laymen's Movement for a Christian World, a committee of sixteen has been appointed to explore the subject in all its aspects. This committee includes six medical doctors, of whom Dr. Frank Sladen, Consultant to Medical Service, Henry Ford Hospital, Detroit, and Dr. Robert Laidlaw of Roosevelt Hospital, New York City, are two. Among its other scientists is Julius Weinberger of the R.C.A. research laboratories.

Concurrently, an objective study of spiritual healing is being conducted by the American Foundation of Religion and Psychology, with which Dr. Smiley Blanton is actively associated. A group of California scientists is presently engaged in an exhaustive research program. In addition to these formal research groups, numerous individual physicians, their interest whetted and curiosity piqued by what they have learned, are privately studying and researching the phenomenon.

All of this investigation indicates medical recognition of the type and number of spiritual healings being reported. Whether it will eventuate in a conclusive report is open to conjecture by a number of both doctors and clergymen. Nevertheless, even if the power of Christ cannot be accurately analyzed in a laboratory and the healing of the human spirit defies the X-ray machine, the value of scientific exploration cannot be overestimated. As products of our mid-twentieth century culture, it is natural enough that we demand a scientific approach.

If for no other reason than to inspire faith in those who disbelieve, scientific confirmation of healings seems vitally important. As a man wonderfully healed of a so-called "fatal" kidney ailment said to me the other day: "You know, if I hadn't known of Dr. Alexis Carrel's experience of seeing a cancer instantly healed before his eyes, I could never have taken spiritual healing seriously." Yes, I knew; for if I hadn't been able to medically substantiate scores of claimed healings, I would have quickly written off the whole subject as superstitious fanaticism.

The last survey on spiritual healing, severely limited in scope by lack of funds, was conducted in 1954 by Dr. Charles Braden of Northwestern University, under the auspices of the then Federal Council of Churches. The findings revealed that sixty-four different types of disease had reportedly been spiritually healed. The largest percentage of healings had occurred in cancer cases, while heart healings followed as a close second.

In some cases these cures were apparently effected as a result of close cooperation between doctors and clergymen. In others, the reported healings had occurred after the doctors had apparently failed. When several outside physicians were asked to comment on the latter group, however, they claimed that the diagnosis had been in error.

Regardless of the documentary evidence of disease and cure, unless a physician has a personal knowledge of the case involved the results of any scientific investigation may well be inconclusive. Doctors frequently differ in their diagnosis of a disease. As one doctor points out, there are few medical men engaged in practice who will accept another's X-rays or laboratory findings. This will hold doubly true when one attempts to compile irrefutable evidence of non-medical cures.

Medical testimonies to instantaneous healings

In cases of instantaneous healings, unless a doctor is on the spot or personally familiar with the case, he will understandably find such cures difficult to credit.

Take the case of a woman in Cleveland who suffered a third degree burn on her right hand. The doctor treated and bandaged the injury in his office. On her way home, she attended a healing service at Emmanuel Episcopal Church, where the Reverend Laurence Blackburn laid his hands lightly on the bandage. As he prayed, the pain in the patient's hand ceased. She felt she had been healed, and returned to her doctor for examination. There remained no sign of the burn except a faint pinkness of the skin. The physician was astounded. He called it a miracle. But would any other, who had not seen the injury just before and just after?

Then there was the woman in Texas who was suffering from an abdominal swelling caused by a tumor so large that it had increased her weight by approximately fifteen pounds. She attended a healing service a few days before she was scheduled to enter the hospital for surgery. When she arose from the altar, her abdomen was as flat as a board. Upon reaching home, she stepped on the scales and found that she had lost over fifteen pounds since early that morning. She went immediately to her doctor, who found no evidence of the tumor. "A higher power has healed you," he said. Would medical investigators be able to accept this type of statement as incontrovertible scientific evidence?

Because of the nature of the subject it would seem that positive findings must come from the increasingly large group of doctors who are actually at the scene of action when medically inexplicable healings occur. The religious-medical combine such as is functioning in Houston may well provide the means for this sort of research. Here the cumulative evidence can be studied and evaluated; for, as one physician says: "It is the massive *cumulative evidence which is so impressive.*"

This is illustrated in St. Peter's Church in Uniontown, Pennsylvania. The Reverend Larned Blatchford, who practices a healing ministry there, reports that nineteen members of the parish underwent major surgery during the past twelve months. In each of these cases malignancy was strongly suspected by the attending physicians. In not one case, however, was malignancy found, nor did any operation prove as serious as had been previously indicated. In every instance a remarkably quick and uneventful recovery took place.

Doctors are increasingly disinclined to dismiss this sort of thing as purely coincidental, just as they are becoming loath to write off as mere coincidence the fact that so many critically ill patients take a dramatic turn for the better at the exact time that prayers are being offered in their behalf.

Cooperation of Doctors with Healing Ministries

Physicians who a short while ago scoffed at the mention of spiritual healing are now working in close cooperation with the churches' healing commissions and clinics. The Healing Commission of the Diocese of Los Angeles, for example, includes a substantial number of doctors; while the Order of St. Luke, an interdenominational healing mission founded ten years ago by the Reverend John Gaynor Banks, includes twenty-five doctors as active members.

Many Christian doctors are now members of prayer groups affiliated with various different churches. St. Stephen's Episcopal Church in Philadelphia numbers half a dozen medical men in its prayer circle, which, divided into groups, prays for the sick at half-hour intervals twenty-one hours a day. In Toledo, Ohio, a powerful healing prayer group has been established and is led by four of the city's leading doctors.

In some areas where the healing ministry is strong, it has become common practice for physicians to send, and sometimes to accompany, their patients to healing services. Occasionally instantaneous healings occur. Frequently the healings are gradual, but doctors report that only rarely does the patient fail to derive obvious benefit from the services. Two doctors to whom I have spoken report that they themselves have been healed instantaneously—one of what had been considered incurable deafness; the other of an incompletely healed fracture where surgical intervention had been distinctly indicated.

Most doctors have conceded that the religious attitude of a patient was an important factor in his recovery. What many are now beginning to understand for the first time is that the *physician's* faith in a healing God can be of immense importance in his healing work. As Dr. William Reed of Bay City, Michigan, observes: "Today there is a new awareness that in the close cooperation between the church and medicine lies a new, great kind of care of illness which brings Christ into His proper place in the thinking and activities of both groups. We are learning through spiritual healing that Christ has a message for physicians which must be listened to."

If I have given the impression that all, or even most, doctors now accept the validity of spiritual healing, I have been in error. Many physicians (but significantly those who know the least about it) react as did a doctor I talked to a few days ago. One of his patients had been diagnosed by means of internal examination, supported by vaginal smear and biopsy, both positive, as having cancer. A complete hysterectomy was scheduled. Before her operation date, she attended several healing services. Convinced that she had received healing, she requested that another smear be taken. It was, and returned negative. A week later another biopsy was performed with the understanding that, were it positive, the hysterectomy would be performed while she was still under the anesthetic. The biopsy was negative; no operation necessary.

When I asked her doctor how he explained this, his answer was typical of nearly all doctors several years ago, but far fewer today: "It's perfectly obvious that she never had cancer," he said. When I asked how he could be so sure in view of the laboratory findings, he replied: "I'm sure, because if she had had cancer, it would still be there. It was all a mistake." It is this sort of reasoning which makes the procurement of medical confirmation both difficult and time-consuming.

It has been my observation in talking to physicians that much of their initial hostility to spiritual healing is due to their mistaken idea that those who believe in spiritual healing don't believe in doctors. Nothing could be further from the truth. The advocates of spiritual healing believe medicine to be a divinely instituted profession. They concur with Dr. Norman Vincent Peale when he says: "The combination of the physician who treats and God who heals is no less a religious process than the cure of souls."

Fully recognizing that the complete healing art comprises three indivisible parts—medical, psychological, and spiritual—those who conduct healing ministries not only urge but insist that those who attend services remain under the care of their doctors. I have noticed that when a physician thoroughly understands this, his antagonism usually diminishes.

I recently had occasion to interview two doctors, both eminent men in their fields, in connection with a medical article

I had in preparation. I had interviewed these same men several years ago in regard to spiritual healing and had found them unequivocally hostile to religious healing of any sort. However, since that time, both had done some investigating. One now voluntarily offered me cases from his files which, he said, "must be termed 'miraculous' as they are medically inexplicable."

The other commented: "Since talking to you last, I have seen many healings of diverse organic and chronic diseases which defy medical explanation. When these healings come as a direct result of prayer, they must, in my opinion, be accepted as miracles."

Dr. Paul Tournier, internationally known French physician, states in his *A Doctor's Casebook* that there is a hierarchy of the person, in which the body is subject to the spirit. With this contention an ever-growing number of physicians, such as Dr. Evarts Loomis of Southern California, agree. "I have noted repeatedly in my practice," he says, "that the extent of a physical healing seems to depend on the change in the spiritual life of the patient which goes with prayer and meditation. On several occasions when a patient was not making satisfactory progress, I have prayed with him either verbally or silently, whether he be Catholic or Protestant, in office or hospital room. Almost invariably, improvement has followed."

Dr. Charles H. Mayo, who conducted an investigation on spiritual healing several years ago, reported: "Christian healing has passed beyond the stage of experiment, and its value cannot be questioned. Spiritual healing no longer is the hope of the few, but the belief and practice of a large and rapidly increasing number of persons."

A steadily growing number of doctors, now familiar with the results of the revived ministry of healing, concede that this is a factual statement.

There is little doubt that we are standing on the threshhold of a new era in the treatment of disease—an era of real Christian faith, which, when coupled with scientific techniques, may well make the *non*-healing of any disease more remarkable than its healing.

It is toward this end that so many dedicated doctors and clergymen are now working. Both use the same text as a basis for their efforts. While the Church fully concurs that "God hath given men skill. . . . With such doth He heal men and taketh away their pains," the doctor, with increasing frequency, asks that his patients "Pray unto the Lord, and He will make thee whole" (*Ecclesiasticus 38:6–8*).

PART **II**

Healing

Ministries

CHAPTER 13

Modern Apostles

$\mathcal{A}$ FEW YEARS AGO, the institution of a healing ministry was a somewhat perilous undertaking. It required the preparation of a congregation probably unused to the idea of spiritual healing.

Today, however, with a widespread general knowledge of the subject, the task of instituting a ministry of healing is far easier. Many clergymen are finding it possible, as did the Reverend Earl Walker, United Lutheran pastor of the Hebron Church in Pittsburg, to begin healing services without prolonged preparation. In his own words: "I just began. I delivered two or three sermons on the healing power of Christ, and then I combined our regular Sunday vespers service with a healing service. My sermons here are based on the Bible and excerpts from various books on healing. After a period of quiet prayer for the sick, I invite any who wish to receive the laying-on-of-hands to come to the altar."

The greatest activity in spiritual healing is usually found in those communities where a leading churchman, of whatever denomination, is keenly interested in the subject. The enthusiasm and support of Bishop Austin Pardue of Pittsburgh, for example, is largely responsible for the leading role this city is playing in the renascence of the healing ministry. Once a ministry has set a precedent, it is easier for others in the locality to "just begin."

The Reverend Harry D. Robinson, Jr., pastor of the Bellmore Methodist Church in Bellmore, Long Island, began his healing ministry by the formation of a healing prayer group. He then sent out a letter to the general church membership in which he asked that they join with him in seeking from God, through group prayer in the church, health and strength for themselves and those they loved. "A prayer group can be as real a tool in God's hand as is the modern hospital," stated the letter. "So I invite you to put another tool in the hand of God: Come and join yourself to a praying group before the altar of our church; come if you are curious, and would like to learn what can happen; come if you are not well, and seek to be well; come if you would help another by your prayers; come and bring someone else who longs for health and wholeness."

Mr. Robinson's weekly healing services include hymns, a message from the Bible, and prayer. Those who wish it receive either the laying-on-of-hands or Holy Unction. Although this is a ministry of only a few months, it has produced many remarkable results.

The Reverend Laurence Blackburn, D.D., Episcopal rector of Emmanuel Church in Cleveland, initiated his notable healing ministry with a mission consisting of a series of eight weekly lectures. He delivered six of these himself and procured two guest speakers well known in the healing field for the remaining two. Each lecture was followed by a question period, and intercessions. The result was a congregation highly literate on the subject of spiritual healing. Services with the laying-on-of-hands were begun the week following the final lecture. Within two months attendance at these weekly services represented thirty-three different churches and nine denominations.

A healing mission is a splendid way to precede the institution of a healing ministry, for it provides a more concentrated and effective "education" in spiritual healing than is possible by an occasional Sunday sermon. If the minister of a church does not feel himself qualified to conduct such a mission personally, he can arrange with someone outstanding in the healing field to deliver the lectures. Where a particular church is small and unable to support such a mission, clergymen of different denominations have cooperated in bringing a missioner to their area. This has proved a fruitful method, for healing ministries have been instituted in as many as five different denominational churches as a result of one series of lectures in one community.

Sunday sermons on healing; the organization of prayer groups; the sending of letters to church members; missions— all these are possible and valuable methods of instigating a healing ministry. Exactly how to begin depends on the individual church. The important thing is to begin.

The Reverend Robert Young of North Presbyterian Church, Pittsburgh, says: "I am ordained, as are all Christian clergy, to preach the Truth, which includes healing. I was called by my congregation to obey God and to lead them in His Holy Ways. I can see no more reason for reluctance in starting a healing ministry than for hesitancy in administering Holy Communion."

The Reverend Young has discovered, as have so many others, that the ministry and their congregations alike can grow in understanding of the healing Christ only after a healing ministry is already functioning, not before it has begun.

Over the past two years, I have seen the beginning of many

new ministries of healing. I have watched increase, not only the spiritual stature of the participating laymen, but the spiritual power of the officiating clergy. These men are indeed today's apostles, handling the power of God as surely as did His first disciples—and with much the same results.

The stories of the individual ministries which follow, are the stories of just a few of the many which are influencing today's revival of spiritual healing. They have been chosen at random. Some are well known; others are not. All, however, are representative of the healing ministry as it functions in various communities and churches over the nation. As each is, in essence, the story of every healing ministry to date, so does each constitute the potential story of every ordained minister in Christendom; for anyone who is authorized to Baptize or to administer Holy Communion or to perform the Sacrament of Marriage is "ready" to undertake the vital ministry of healing which is so inherent and inseparable a part of the Church's whole ministry.

Some of the following clergymen have an undeniable healing gift; others have not. It is perhaps significant that none was aware of this gift until he began his healing work. But the absence or presence of a charismatic gift is immaterial. The clergy cannot, nor does it ever profess, to heal. It serves only as a channel for Christ's healing power, as it is mediated through the Church.

A glance at these healing ministries makes it clear that God mediates His power under varying circumstances and in different surroundings. As the Reverend William Holmes, well known for his healing work in New Mexico, confesses with admirable candor: "It took me a long time to realize the foolishness and egotism of trying to bottle up almighty God in my own limited and conventional thought molds. But at long last I have learned no longer to distrust or disdain the manifestations of spiritual power and healing which come outside my own familiar path."

All of us who believe in the healing Christ owe an incalculable debt of gratitude to our twentieth-century apostles of healing. They are the spokesmen for Christ who are not only eloquently re-articulating, but reaffirming with "signs" the tremendous truth that God loves us and that nothing, not things past or things to come or even we, ourselves, can separate us from His love. Through the working of the Holy Spirit they are leading the way to a new era in Christianity—a rebirth of its pristine power, founded on a vibrant faith in the living God.

CHAPTER 14

The Reverend Alfred W. Price

(*Episcopal*)

ONE HAS only to step inside the beautiful old church of St. Stephen, in the heart of Philadelphia, to recognize it as a true sanctuary of healing, a center of living faith, filled with the presence of the Holy Spirit.

The inspired leader of this "powerhouse of the love of Christ" is a six-foot-four ex-marine, holder of a Purple Heart from World War I, and for many years the national chaplain of the Military Order of the Purple Heart. As gentle as he is strong, as compassionate as he is huge, Dr. Alfred W. Price is a true apostle of faith and love, whose healing ministry has exerted an immeasurable influence on churches of all denominations.

It all began for him in 1942, shortly after he had assumed the rectorship of St. Stephen's Episcopal Church. Searching for a way to help more effectively the many who came to him in mental, spiritual, and often physical distress, he providentially came across a small leaflet which, as he says, "was actually to precipitate me into the healing ministry."

This pamphlet contained a description of the revived emphasis on physical healing which fell within the province of the historic ministry, and related the success of several ministers in the laying-on-of-hands. As he finished reading it, Dr. Price recalled that when he was a student theologian, he had heard Dr. Richard Cabot, of Harvard Medical School, contend that ministers could be doing three-quarters of the healing work of physicians, and doing it better.

Still pondering the matter the next morning, Dr. Price went into the church to pray for guidance. He opened his Bible to James 5:14: "Is any sick among you? let him call for the elders of the Church; and let them pray over him, anointing him with oil in the name of the Lord."

The words he had read so many times before were now fraught with new meaning. When he arose from his knees, he had made his decision.

From his pulpit the next Sunday Alfred Price invited anyone interested in healing to attend a special noon service the following Thursday. Thus began a ministry of such spiritual power as to attract the attention of both clergy and laity across the nation—a ministry which has served as an example for churches everywhere.

Early in his healing ministry, Dr. Price learned that when the Sacrament of Holy Communion was used at the healing services of a large city church such as St. Stephen's, it tended to keep members of other faiths, or of no faith, from the services. "It seemed to me a barrier, preventing many needy people from joining us," explained Dr. Price. "We therefore discontinued this Sacrament at the healing services. They now consist of a sermon based strictly on the New Testament, and the laying-on-of-hands."

The rector devotes every Thursday wholly to the healing

ministry, "in order," he says, "to do justice to the clear command of Our Lord to heal the sick."

He counsels by appointment throughout the day in preparation for the two healing services held at 12:30 and 5:30 in the afternoon. These are attended by approximately four hundred people of all faiths and none, of all races, rich and poor, united briefly as they kneel before the altar in their common need.

Some of these supplicants come from far away. A number have been sent to the healing services by their doctors, and a few physicians sit in the pews with their patients.

Scores of organic, functional, and mental diseases have been healed at St. Stephen's. "We have discovered," says Dr. Price, "that there is no disease that is incurable, and no problem which cannot be solved when God is allowed to take over."

Some of these healings have been instantaneous, as was the case with a woman whose hand was swollen to three times its normal size with arthritis. Immediately after she received the healing sacrament and prayer, her hand returned to its natural size, completely cured. The patient has dedicated this now useful hand to the service of the Lord.

Some healings, rather than "instantaneous," might be called "immediate," as in the case of a spastic baby carried to the high altar by Dr. Price, while her family knelt in prayer at the altar rail.

"The child felt like jelly in my arms," relates Dr. Price. "There was no coordination of arms or limbs. While I prayed, the baby suddenly started to cry with loud, piercing screams."

She continued to cry for two days. The family, frantic with anxiety, called the clergyman, who expressed his opinion that the healing was taking place. "So many experience this same distress," says Dr. Price, "while the battle for healing is going on."

When the infant finally stopped crying and slept, the miracle had taken place. She was completely cured. Today she is a healthy, robust child.

But many healings come more slowly, as did that of a three-year-old child, crippled with a club foot. His right foot was almost completely imbedded in the leg, but after six months of attendance at healing services, the child was completely healed.

The healing of a man with a medically diagnosed cancer of the bone didn't take quite so long. Scheduled for radical surgery, the patient received the sacraments of healing several times. The pain grew less each time he received the rites with prayer, until he was finally free of all discomfort. X-rays revealed what his doctor termed a "miraculous regeneration of the bone."

But however great the physical need, and however wonderful the healings, Dr. Price never lets us forget the necessity of placing disease in the perspective of man's total need, and healing in the context of God's total gift. "The Christian ideal is to have a God-filled personality not for health's sake, but for God's sake."

Nor does he pretend that it is simple to fulfil the essential conditions upon which healing usually depends. "Absolute relinquishment of self and personal ambition is never easy," he remarks. "Nor is it easy to lose one's resentment, and to make thankfulness a constant habit of our minds. But when people go all out to do these things, I have seen the healing power of God rush in with the force of a Niagara river and literally recreate every cell, every tissue, every organ; renew the whole personality—body, mind, and spirit."

The dignity and complete lack of sensationalism of the St. Stephen's services, the powerful support of those dedicated members of the healing Prayer Fellowship; the sound theological approach and deep spirituality of Dr. Price have proved to many ministers and laymen who had reservations that spiritual healing is indeed a revival of an honored and traditional ministry of the Church.

The Price ministry illumines for all to see what he believes to be the heart of the Gospel: "that the power of the Holy Spirit is within us to heal, to inspire, and to give life."

Before he lays on hands, Dr. Price faces the altar and, with out-stretched arms, prays this great prayer of consecration: "O Lord, take my mind and think through it. Take my heart and set it on fire with love. Take these hands and through them bring to these thy suffering children, the fullness of thy healing power."

Again and again we see this prayer answered; for although Dr. Price makes clear that all are not physically healed, there are few indeed who leave the altar rail unaware of His Presence.

It is said that St. Stephen's Church was the first in Philadelphia to be electrically lit. The light that streams from her now cannot be measured in watts. Penetrating fifteen hundred centuries of darkness, its gleam has pointed the way to a knowledge of Him and of His truth that can transform the world.

CHAPTER 15

The Reverend Richard E. Winkler

(*Episcopal*)

$\mathcal{R}$ICHARD WINKLER, rector of Trinity Episcopal Church in the Chicago suburb of Wheaton, began his ministry of healing less than five years ago when a small group of interested persons began meeting to study prayer in all its phases, and to make intercession for the sick and needy.

"But as I look back now," comments the clergyman, "I think I have always believed in the principles of Christian healing."

Mr. Winkler and his wife, Dorothy, were married eleven years before he was ordained. During that time they saw several dramatic healings take place as a result of prayer. One which touched them closely concerned a member of the family who after a serious automobile accident was hospitalized with broken ribs, a broken vertebra, and a pelvis fractured in three places.

"Prayers were offered by our rector," Mr. Winkler relates, "and a rapid recovery resulted, her time schedule for the healing process being about half as long all the way through as that established by her doctors. One cannot be as close as this to such a healing without being deeply impressed by God's great love and healing power."

One case in Mr. Winkler's early ministry, involved a man whose doctors had given him six months to live following surgery for intestinal cancer. Prayers were offered daily for his recovery, and his condition steadily improved. Six months beyond his expected time to live, he returned to his physican for examination. The doctor was astounded to find him recovered. Today, four years later, he is alive and well, doing work which involves strenuous physical labor.

The faith of the prayer group grew as the members saw continual evidence of the power of the healing Christ, manifested not only in physical cures, or the rapid healings of emotional and mental problems, but in those healings of the spirit which led to conversion.

"It is true," reports Mr. Winkler, "That in the beginning my parish was wary of spiritual healing. I am sure that a large number suspected this, to them new, ministry of mysticism or even some spiritism. But through our prayer group there has been a steady educational process and a leavening growth among the parishioners; so that today in Trinity Church this ministry to the sick is accepted as a normal part of the parish life. Requests for prayers for healing now come from persons who would not have thought of making them a few years ago; and healing services are attended regularly by members of the parish who do not participate in the Prayer Group."

The Trinity Prayer Group is organized as a chapter of the Order of St. Luke. It includes Presbyterians, Congregationalists, Baptists, and others, as well as Episcopalians from nearby parishes, many of whom are members of similar groups in their own church. About one-third of the membership are men, and a number of young married couples are regular attendants at the meetings.

The regular Thursday night meeting of the group closes with a healing service in the Church, with prayers, hymns, and the laying-on-of-hands.

"We have found," states Mr. Winkler, "that the power of the Holy Spirit works in a marvelous way during these healing services held in conjunction with the Prayer Group meeting."

But the clergyman feels a need for the Holy Communion in Christ's healing work; so in addition to the Thursday night healing services he has instituted a weekly celebration of the Lord's Supper, followed by the healing rites. At this service sitters are available for young mothers who wish to attend, but a number of children prefer to take part in the worship and even come to the altar for the laying-on-of-hands.

Mr. Winkler has found that this is the service most frequently attended by visitors from other churches. It is followed by a coffee hour in the Parish Hall, "and it is here," says the minister, "that a great many visitors are introduced to the enthusiasm felt by those who have been active in the work of Christian healing." Through the healing ministry at Trinity, the Holy Spirit has touched and changed the lives of many.

It is a regular and now-expected occurrence that a physical change takes place at almost the same time as prayers for recovery are being offered, as in the case of a hospitalized patient suffering the excruciating pain of gall stones. Within the hour that prayers were said in her behalf, the pain ceased. The patient returned home the next morning, the scheduled surgery canceled.

Through prayers and the healing services, recoveries from all kinds of illnesses are invariably speeded far beyond the doctors' prognostications. Not a few are the spectacular healings which serve to build continually higher the faith of the Church.

A few weeks ago, for example, a woman in her sixties, suffering from a severe phlebitis, which prevented her from walking without the aid of a cane and made it impossible for her to bend her knees, attended the Tuesday morning healing service. Receiving Holy Communion, she suddenly found herself kneeling at the altar rail for the first time in twenty-two years. After the laying-on-of-hands, she walked a mile to her home, leaving her cane in the church.

Another thrilling healing was that of a patient who had suffered a coronary occlusion with severe damage to the heart muscle. The medical prognosis was poor, and an indefinite period of complete bedrest was recommended. Prayers were offered for her, and she received the laying-on-of-hands three times while in bed. After each time a decided improvement was noted. The improvement confirmed by electrocardiogram, the patient was permitted out of bed in just two weeks, and is now living a normal life with a grateful and healthy heart. She is, incidentally, seventy-seven years old!

But, as the Reverend Winkler emphasizes, it is the healing of the spirit, not of the body or mind, which is of primary importance. In this connection he cites the case of a man and wife who dramatically illustrate the totality of Christ's healing power.

This couple, not members of the Church, were referred to his prayer group for help. Their case was already in the divorce courts; the wife had been emotionally disturbed for some time, and the husband was the victim of serious ailments of both stomach and heart. Shortly after prayers were offered for this couple, a singular change came over their lives. The divorce suit was dropped; they were reconciled; and both were completely healed physically as well as spiritually. Members of no church until that time, they joined one in their community. The wife has organized an effective prayer group; the husband devotes much of his time to making hospital calls, and has encouraged a number of his associates to do the same.

"Just another of the many cases," comments Mr. Winkler,

"where redeemed lives have gone on to witness God's healing power to others."

The clergyman also describes a personal situation which I have found characteristic of the results of participation in the healing ministry, whether as layman or minister. His three sons, aged thirteen, eleven, and two years, have never suffered a childhood sickness, regardless of exposure. This Mr. Winkler attributes to the protective power of God, to whom each day in perfect faith he commits his family. "Naturally we believe in medicine," he says, "but we also believe first in prayer at the slightest sign of illness."

Richard Winkler's experience with spiritual healing also typifies in another area the experience of the healing clergy everywhere. "As I look over my parish," he says, "and see the Holy Spirit at work in the lives of so many persons, I can say that most of the true conversions to Jesus Christ have come through the healing ministry."

This ministry at Trinity is impressive evidence of the power of the Holy Spirit to heal and to convert. This is the witness of the healing Church, providing the Christian world's best hope for triumph over the antichrist.

CHAPTER 16

The Reverend Charles A. Sumners

(*Episcopal*)

$\mathcal{W}$HEN I discussed the beginnings of his fine healing ministry with Mr. Sumners of St. David's Episcopal Church in Austin, Texas, the clergyman smiled rather ruefully and remarked: "I'm afraid this reflects the course of a number of ministers who, along with me, showed a very hesitant approach toward the acceptance of responsibility."

But hesitancy a few years ago was understandable. There was then little knowledge of the Church's healing ministry, and the whole movement might well have proved a wild flight of fancy on the part of a few fanatics. It is in great measure to painstaking theologians like Mr. Sumners that we owe the Church's increasingly widespread acceptance of spiritual healing today, for it was his concern with the theological validity of the healing ministry which dictated his caution. His prolonged study of the ministry eventually convinced him of its integrity and rightful place in the Church's entire ministry.

Mr. Sumners has been interested in healing longer than most clergymen to whom I have talked, for it was during his university days that he made a study of the "Emmanuel Movement," begun in 1906 by the Reverend Elwood Worcester at Emmanuel Church in Boston. This was the first rational and practical application of the psychological method to the problem of religion. Although it died out at the death of its founder, its influence is again evident in ministries such as that of Dr. Norman Vincent Peale, who uses much the same psychiatric-psychological-religious approach to spiritual healing.

Throughout his years at seminary Mr. Sumners maintained his interest. After his ordination he became increasingly convinced that the work of Christian healing was integral in the Church's life, and should be utilized as a regular part of the Church's ministry to her people.

"At the same time," the clergyman pointed out, "I felt the necessity of being on absolutely sound ground Scripturally and theologically before inaugurating this work."

Continuous New Testament study was to bring Mr. Sumners added conviction, as were the accounts of other healing ministries which were by then available.

"But," he says, "I confess with shame that I was more concerned, first with being theologically sound, and then with the attitude of my fellow-clergy, than I was with the undertaking of a great venture of faith in the Name of Our Lord and Saviour, Jesus Christ. For even after I became convinced that this was the work of the Church and that the Church ought to undertake such a mission with courage and determination, it was still eight or nine years after I became rector of St. David's that I actually held a service of Divine healing."

The Reverend Sumners enumerated for me those four basic factors which finally made the institution of healing services seem imperative.

First, the unchangeableness of God. Either the New Testament is in error, or Jesus Christ performed mighty acts. If He did then, He can now.

Second, the unassailable fact of the practice of the healing ministry throughout the Church's long history. Healing services today are continuous with the tradition of the Church.

Third, all healing comes from God. Without question His healing mercy comes through medicine as well as the healing Sacraments; but no logical reason could suggest that the sacramental life of the Church should be excluded.

Fourth is the fact of modern man's need for healing of soul, mind, and body. The Church has a unique opportunity to bring to humankind a healing grace which at times may be supportive, at times primary, but at all times spiritual and sacramental for man's whole being.

When Charles Sumners made his decision to inaugurate a healing ministry, he had no precedent in his section of Texas. At just about the same time, however, and for the same basic reasons, another such ministry was to begin—that of Charles' twin brother, the Reverend Thomas Sumners of the Church of St. John the Divine in Houston. Both ministries have now been in operation nearly nine years.

The first of the weekly healing services at St. David's in Austin took place on July 1, 1948, and its format has not changed over the years. Following the service of Holy Communion, Mr. Sumners goes to the Prayer Desk in the Chancel for meditation on some fundamental aspect of the Christian faith. The subject of the meditation is often determined by questions which have been recently asked by members of the congregation. Following this period are the intercessions. Only Christian names are used, and the ailments for which prayers are desired are never mentioned. "If they are," says Mr. Sumners, "the ailment frequently becomes the center of thought, and not the mighty action of God, who, in full measure, knows the real difficulty."

After the list of names is read, with frequent pauses for thanksgiving to God for His healing action *now*, those who desire the laying-on-of-hands proceed to the Communion rail. The priest goes to the altar for a prayer of thanksgiving and consecration before he administers the healing Sacrament.

"Although we do not deny that God indeed endows certain individuals with special gifts of healing," states Mr. Sumners, "I think it extremely important that people realize that the efficacy of the healing service is not dependent upon any man, but upon the Sacraments. For this reason we make it a point to have my associate, the Reverend Albert Walling, sometimes assist with the laying-on-of-hands, and occasionally to take the entire service. By doing this, we affirm our conviction concerning the sacramental nature of God's healing action in and through His Church."

When I asked Mr. Sumners to tell me something of the physical results of his healing ministry, he was inclined to dismiss the question as irrelevant. Nevertheless, the list is long of people whose spiritual lives have been affected by the healing ministry at St. David's, and who have received obvious and definable physical benefits.

A young man, for example, faced a radical operation for a cancerous colon condition. After receiving the laying-on-of-hands, he was not only physically healed by the power of God so that surgery was unnecessary, but, as a result of his experience, underwent a marked personality change. He is now happily married and a tireless worker in the Church. Such was the case, also, with a woman who faced an operation for breast cancer. The growth miraculously disappeared shortly before the scheduled radical mastectomy.

Then there was the dying child who received the laying-on-of-hands at midnight in his hospital crib and immediately took a dramatic turn for the better. He is today in perfect health. And the woman in her late forties who suffered a severe back and hip injury as the result of a fall. In continual pain, controllable only by sedatives, she attended a healing service, was immediately relieved of all pain and discomfort, and filled as well with the God-given vitality which is hers to-day.

"There are, of course, failures in healing which we cannot explain," comments Mr. Sumners. "All we can do is continue to try through diligent prayer and study to become a more effective instrument of his power and grace. However, I have never administered the Sacrament at any time or in any condition where a lack of physical improvement resulted in disappointment or despair."

During our interview Mr. Sumners suggested that his early conservatism in regard to spiritual healing may have placed him in the category of those condemned by Our Lord: "Neither will they believe though one rose from the dead." If this should be so, his present ministry of healing has surely redeemed him!

The healing ministry at St. David's reflects the humility, the love, and the faith of its administrant, filled now with the deep and abiding feeling that the mighty action of God revealed in Christ Jesus awaits only the mighty action of men who will respond; convinced that those who dare to believe in God's healing grace must act in His Name.

CHAPTER 17

The Reverend Edgar N. Jackson

(*Methodist*)

𝒯HE HEALING MINISTRY of the Reverend Jackson, of the Mamaroneck, New York, Methodist Church, is particularly interesting because of the pastor's own strongly scientific background and his unusually close association with the medical profession. By virtue of his extensive experience as a hospital chaplain, his membership on a committee studying psychosomatic medicine and spiritual healing, and his present position as administrative head of a clinic, his healing ministry forms a uniquely effective liaison between spiritual healing and medicine.

Pastor Jackson originally studied to be an engineer. When as a very young man he was first confronted with the healing power of prayer, he was torn two ways. The circumstantial evidence of healing was impressive, but his scientific training had, as he says, "instilled in me a good dose of healthy skepti-

cism. I demanded a logical answer for everything." After he
ultimately decided to eschew an engineering career and follow in his clergyman father's footsteps, he was to find that
answer.

As a chaplain in a mental hospital he first observed the impact of thought and feeling on the functioning of the physical
organism. Full realization of the enormous extent to which
human emotions could influence the body, causing physical
disease of all kinds, came to him during the war when he
served as base chaplain at a replacement center. Here he sat in
on the daily hospital staff meetings, where cases were discussed in detail. He learned first hand of the immeasurably
destructive effects of fear and anxiety on strong bodies. Again
and again he saw patients referred to the psychiatrist or chaplain for care, rather than to the surgeon or the doctor of internal medicine.

The impact of his early witness to the healing power of God
had never wholly left him. By the end of the war, Mr. Jackson had organized several healing prayer groups for intercession, with exceedingly rewarding results. But he was eager to
learn more of the science of human personality. Enrolling in
a postgraduate center for psychotherapy, the clergyman pur-
sued his studies, the only minister among a large number of
physicians and psychiatrists.

This experience provided an unexcelled opportunity for
him to check carefully his ideas on spiritual healing against
the best medical judgments of the day. As he puts it: "Being
exposed to other professional healing disciplines made me
examine carefully the bases of procedure in any activity that
had to do with the complicated structure of human personality. But while caution is desirable in any field dealing with
the human soul, I concluded that caution should stem from
that basic concern, and not from *fear in employing an adventurous faith.* I undertook my healing ministry fully convinced
that there are resources available to the clergyman by tradition and practice, which are vitally necessary to complete

health, but which obviously cannot be a part of the physician's practice."

Mr. Jackson emphasizes the substantial number of doctors who are in full agreement with this premise, and for this reason are now cooperating to the fullest extent with their colleagues among the clergy.

"Many of these," the minister comments, "accept the soul theory as defined in traditional religious terms, and not a few recognize the influence of spiritual healing. Though they can not understand all that is involved, they have verified what has taken place through medical examinations before and after."

One such case was a healing for an inflammatory skin disease, received by a woman who had been under a specialist's care for many months. Prayers were offered for her at the healing service, and a few days later Mr. Jackson received a telephone call from her physician.

"Mrs. X has just been in for her weekly treatment," said the doctor. "She appears completely cured. What on earth did you do for her at the church?" When told of the group prayer, he readily agreed that this must have been an important factor in her recovery.

The surgeon who operated on Mr. Y outspokenly refers to the patient's complete recovery as a "miracle."

Mr. Y was scheduled for a severe heart operation which involved the freezing of the body. A prayer vigil was arranged for the day of the operation. During surgery the heart stopped beating and did not function for eighteen minutes. When the heart action was restored, there was acute danger of loss of mental competence through lack of oxygen supply to the brain. Not only was the operation successful, but there was no sign of impaired function, and full recovery ensued.

In discussing these and many other similar healings, Mr. Jackson pointed out the variables which exist. Some patients, for example, knew they were being prayed for, and had the feeling of group support which in and of itself was clearly beneficial. Others, however, did not know they were the subject of prayer, and the group support factor did not enter in. One such instance concerned an alcoholic of long standing who, a year ago and unknown to him, was held in prayer at a healing service at the request of his wife. The following day he stopped drinking—without explanation—and has not had a drink since.

Pastor Jackson told me of other cases where the persons healed disavowed all faith in God, but either reluctantly agreed to attend a healing service or to permit the prayer group to pray for them. Such an instance was that of a woman who had had an operation for cancer. Faced with another, she was distraught, claimed no belief in God, and contemplated suicide. A member of no church, she rather unwillingly agreed to permit the Mamaroneck group to pray for her. When she reported for the pre-operative examination, shortly after prayers had been offered in her behalf, there was no evidence of the growth.

In reporting her physical situation before and after the healing, her doctor declared that the malignancy had not only been arrested, but had disappeared. Twenty-one months later, after repeated examinations, the patient showed no evidence of the growth. Her healing, as is almost invariably the case with unbelievers, resulted in her conversion. She has joined a church and organized a prayer group in the community in which she now lives.

Pastor Jackson comments that in some healings the illness was so clearly psychogenic in nature that a change in attitude was sufficient to explain any beneficial results.

"But we quickly move beyond the realm of easy explanation," says the clergyman, "when we see healings where an actual change of tissue is involved. It seems to me clear that the spiritual nature of man cannot be limited by explanation."

Believing that life is a spiritual fact, a point of view that has much support from modern science at this point, Mr. Jackson, through his healing ministry strives to be a channel for the healing and redeeming love of God. Through his ministry, he is seeking to live and practice the nature of God that was revealed in the life and teaching of Jesus.

"This," he says, "is not so much a philosophy as it is a way of life, rooted in a daring and adventurous faith. We do not so much seek to *have* a faith, as to *be* a faith. We do not so much seek to love in the abstract as to love in the concrete relations of life that engage us."

The healing services at Mamaroneck Church are simple and ritualistic, consisting of Scripture reading, a short meditation, the laying-on-of-hands, and prayer.

"Our praying," explains Mr. Jackson, "is not a medical exercise, not an assault on symptoms. Rather it is a determined effort to release life from the ideas that constrict and destroy it. In this way we do not interfere with any other form of healing that may be employed. We support it, supplement it, and move *beyond* it to the spiritual nature of man where true health is found. For we remember well the words of Jesus, 'Your faith has made you well.' "

When I asked the Reverend Jackson what he felt to be his primary purpose as a minister of Jesus Christ, he answered: "To help persons grow to an adventurous faith that helps to bring them wholeness of being."

This, I think, comes close to what Jesus meant when He promised a more abundant life.

CHAPTER 18

The Reverend John H. Parke

(*Episcopal*)

S PIRITUAL HEALING has never been a new concept to John Parke, the young rector of St. James Episcopal Church, Newport Beach, California; for his clergyman father was marvelously healed of tuberculosis when John was a small boy. Brought up in a home where, as he says, "the idea of healing through prayer and Sacraments was as natural as the air we breathed," it is scarcely surprising that Mr. Parke should have considered healing a regular part of his total ministry. His belief was even further strengthened by a deep spiritual experience underwent while serving as Chaplain for the 261st Infantry in France.

Just after the Battle of the Bulge, the end of January, 1945, the regiment was encamped in the mud at Camp Lucky Strike, not far from Le Havre. Mr. Parke, along with many of his men, had succumbed to what was called "atypical" pneumonia; and after running a fever of 105 degrees for two days in a field tent, he was taken to a hospital in Dieppe.

Father Parke recalls that "after taking a great handful of sulpha pills in the afternoon," he fell into a sort of delirium around seven P.M., having a feeling he was hovering between heaven and hell, and very close to death. He remembers that around eight o'clock a nurse came in to take his pulse and temperature, and, as she left the room, she snapped out the light, leaving the door open just a crack.

"The next moment," relates the clergyman, "I had the most extraordinary experience of my life. A strange, ghostly light began pouring in from that crack, moved up toward the ceiling, then along the wall and directly toward me. I got up on one elbow and stared at this thing, terrified. Then with a feeling that this was some sort of angel of death approaching me, I began a rhythmic prayer, 'Jesus be with me' with every breath.

"As I prayed, the shapeless light retreated, but then, as fear returned, so did this apparition. I then decided to lie down, relax, and close my eyes, continuing the prayer. My heart was beating like a trip-hammer, and I was conscious that the light was now hovering right over me.

"Suddenly three ice-cold shocks wracked my body, followed by a flood of warmth, and I felt Our Lord's actual Presence with me more vividly than ever before or since in my life. The breathing came easier now. I could sense that the light was receding, and finally was gone, although I didn't open my eyes to look. My rhythmic prayer now became, 'Jesus, be with me forever.'

"A few minutes later the nurse returned, switched on the light, and, looking at me sharply, remarked; 'What's happened to you?' I simply smiled and said, 'I'll be all right now.'

"I slept soundly, and the next morning had a normal temperature. Ever since that time I have had more than an academic belief in the power of prayer. I have felt a deep certainty."

Mr. Parke's first healing experience was with sick children, for early in his ministry he discovered how responsive to prayer is the subconscious of a child, and how readily released in children is the healing power of God.

He mentions, for example, the times within the past year that he has received frantic calls from parents, saying that their new-born child had congestion of the lungs, and was given less than a fifty-fifty chance to live.

"Each time," reports Father Parke, "I felt I could meet the situation with confidence, first reassuring the mother, asking her to relax and just surround her baby with love, releasing it to God's loving care. Then donning a mask and gown, I went into the hospital nursery, looked down on the infant, set my breathing in harmony with the child's, visualized the lungs becoming clear, and thanked God for His healing power. In every case the child was out of danger within the hour."

Just a few weeks ago the clergyman received a call from another distraught mother. Her little girl, eighteen months old, was convalescing from pneumonia. Through vomiting and diarrhea, the child had become completely dehydrated and refused to eat or drink. She was receiving intravenous feeding in the hospital, but was making no progress. Her condition was precarious. "I laid on hands with the prayer of faith," says Mr. Parke. "Within half an hour the child took a bowl of Jello and, to the amazement of the nurses, began eating with normal appetite."

In every parish in which he has served since the war, Father Parke has instituted a healing ministry and organized a supporting prayer group, the members of which he personally selects. His weekly healing service on Thursday is invariably preceded by a prayer group meeting, after which he administers Holy Communion, followed by the laying-on-of-hands with anointing for those who desire it. Sometimes those who receive the sacramental rites are praying for themselves, but often they are seeking healing for someone else, for, Father Parke comments, "we find that the healing Sacraments received with special intention for the sick give added power to the intercessor."

An example of this is the healing of a woman suffering from cancer of the colon and an intestinal blockage. The clergyman was called to the hospital on a Thursday afternoon to see the sick woman. She appeared amazingly cheerful. "The doctor says I'm going to be fine," she announced jubilantly. "And the blockage passed this morning at about ten o'clock."

Father Parke made no comment, but noted that that was just the time the prayer group was praying for her. "I was reminded," he said to me, "of those passages in the Gospels: 'It was at the seventh hour the fever left him.' "

For a period of several weeks, there appeared among the other communicants at St. James's altar rail, an Eskimo from an Episcopal Mission in Alaska. The young man had been wounded by a polar bear several months before, and had suffered exposure for three days during a blizzard. As a consequence of this experience, he had developed a crippling arthritis. Sent to the warm climate of California in the hope that this would help him, he learned of the healing ministry at the Newport Beach Church. He traveled many miles by bus to attend services and received the Sacrament of Unction. He ascribes his healing progress to the power of God, channeled through this Sacrament, rather than to the change of climate.

Not long ago he stood on the steps of St. James's and read the notice of the Thursday healing service on the church's signboard. Smiling, he nodded his approval. "I wish I could see that sign everywhere," he said.

"Some day" remarked Father Parke, "I think he will."

CHAPTER 19

The Reverend Crawford W. Brown

(*Episcopal*)

D̲r̲. B̲r̲o̲w̲n̲ has established a notable healing ministry at the Church of Our Saviour, San Gabriel, California, where he assumed his present post as rector in 1953. Equally well known for his outstanding healing work in Washington, D.C., where he served as Canon of Washington Episcopal Cathedral for five years, it is fitting that he should be Chairman of the Healing Commission of the Diocese of Los Angeles.

Dr. Brown is an eloquent spokesman for the theological validity of the healing ministry.

"Healing," he emphasizes, "is not something that the Protestant Episcopal Church has suddenly become enamoured with. It is not something that has of this moment been given to the Church by an Act of both Houses of General Convention. It is an integral part of the corporate life and worship of the Church of Jesus Christ. It is sacramental, and, further, it was central in the life and teaching of Our Lord; and, as such, the Church has received the same."

This eminent Episcopal clergyman reminds us that in Jesus Christ, God invaded history with power and with great glory. "This should be a glorious truth to all who profess Christianity and who call upon Jesus Christ as their Saviour and Lord.

"But when" he asks, "will this mighty truth grip and hold Christians everywhere, the clergy as well as the laity?"

Immediately after Dr. Brown came to the San Gabriel Church five years ago he organized the Prayer Fellowship which has so strongly supported his healing ministry there. Ever since then, this prayer chain has been operating eighteen hours a day, each member being responsible for fifteen minutes of prayer for the sick. Thousands of names are prayed for each year, requests being sent or called in from members of all churches.

The healing services are conducted without fanfare or publicity, except for a weekly notice that each Wednesday there is a Service of Holy Communion, with prayers and the laying-on-of-hands.

"The power of the Holy Spirit," says Dr. Brown, "has eloquently testified to the validity of all that is done and said here."

This would seem abundantly true, for God's power has reached down and touched many at these services.

Of the numerous healings which have occurred under Dr. Brown's ministry, one, the personal testimony of a well-known doctor, is offered here in full, as he gave it to me:

"Physicians have long recognized the close tie between spiritual and physical healing. Most of us appreciate the fact that when physical healing ends, it is possible for spiritual healing to complete the process.

"In my own case I was in a Naval hospital suffering with far advanced pulmonary tuberculosis. Specialists in this disease know that the patient goes through four stages before he may recover.

"The first stage is that of shock. He cannot quite realize what has happened to him, and the full import of his personal catastrophe has not yet impressed him.

"The second stage is a feeling of great depression. His whole world has collapsed around his feet, and the world looks very dark indeed.

"The third stage is that of resentment or belligerence. Why should this horrible disease afflict him? He knows his friends and associates are continuing their daily existence in good health, but he is confined to bed for a year or more.

"The fourth stage is that of hope. Perhaps there is a chance that he will get well—a chance that he may be able to resume his normal life if he spends the required time in bed, and if the medicines are effective in curing his disease.

"It is in this fourth and final stage that the spiritual healing plays such an important part in completing the cure of the body.

"My wife was invited by her mother to attend a healing service conducted by the Reverend Crawford Brown. She was so impressed by this service that she immediately telephoned me at the hospital and told me the hour at which these services were conducted weekly. I decided to take part in them, although from a great distance. By praying for help in regaining my health, perhaps our combined efforts would be of benefit to me. Amazingly enough, from that day on, my physical condition improved remarkably, and my spiritual health soared.

"One afternoon after I was permitted to be up, I was watching a telecast of a baseball game in the officer's lounge. I was joined by a Navy chaplain who was undergoing tests for tuberculosis. At the end of the inning he turned to me and said: 'Doctor, you take care of the bodies, and I take care of the souls. Let's get our bodies and souls together and go over to the sick ward and see if we can do some good.' How true his philosophy, and how effective could be our combined talents.

"When I returned home for convalescence, I was able to attend in person Dr. Brown's healing services. On each occasion I could feel health flowing into my body from his hands placed upon my head; and, hearing his prayers, I knew the power of spiritual help in healing my body."

This doctor, who has himself experienced the Presence and healing of the Holy Spirit, could understand the remarkable, instantaneous eye healing received by a high-school girl. Absent from school for a month because of a serious eye ailment, this girl heard of the healing services at Dr. Brown's church and decided to attend. So certain was she of healing that she took her school books with her to the church, planning to go straight on to school. After the laying-on-of-hands and prayer, she was indeed ready to proceed to school—for she found herself perfectly healed.

Dr. Brown stands convinced that the essential ministry of the Church is comprehended in Our Lord's command to teach, preach, baptize, and pray. He challenges all clergy everywhere when he says: "It is incumbent upon the clergy of the Church of the Living God to bring to the attention of all the people committed to their care the philosophies, the aims, the objectives, the faith, the Sacraments, and the True Word of the Living God, whose command of nearly two thousand years ago still rings in our ears. There is a terrific heart and soul hunger for spiritual nourishment; and only by feeding the whole man, body, mind, and spirit, with spiritual food that is available, will we be able to 'down' some of the rampant humanism and materialism, and quench some of the fears that sting men worse than the 'fiery darts of the devil.' "

The rector of Our Saviour makes clear that the reply of Jesus to the Sadducees is as relevant today as when it was first spoken.

"The same day came to him the Sadducees, which say that there is no resurrection. . . . Jesus answered and said unto them, Ye do err, not knowing the Scriptures, nor the power of God" (*Matthew 22:23–29*).

The Church is now charged with His Presence and with His power. Dr. Brown asks a cogent question of both clergy and laity: "Will we recognize the Presence—and will we use the power?"

CHAPTER 20

The Reverend Richard Rettig

(*United Church of Christ*)

When one of his seminary professors heard that Dr. Rettig of St. Peter's United Church of Christ,* Pittsburgh, had begun a healing ministry, he was astounded. "Not Rettig of all people!" he gasped. This was the general reaction of all who knew this clergyman, for Richard Rettig, outstanding intellectual, had made a name for himself throughout the Church as a modernist and liberalist of the first order.

"I attended a conservative seminary, which my father had attended before me," he relates, "but modernism was in the air, and I absorbed it like a sponge. I well remember the distress of my professors when I argued for a liberal interpretation of accepted doctrine. And curiously enough, I, of all

* This denomination is the result of a recently-effected union of the Evangelical Reformed and Congregational Christian Churches.

my class, was the only one to depart from the 'faith once and for all delivered to the saints.' "

When Richard Rettig graduated from seminary he had, as he says now, "all the answers, intellectually, but I had nothing whatsoever to give to the hungry soul. My mind came between me and God, and although I never would have admitted it then, the truth was that I was spiritually bankrupt."

For years Dr. Rettig preached a liberal Gospel, adeptly explaining away the miracles of Jesus. "Those I couldn't put aside so easily," he recalls, "I just never preached about."

It was four successive breakdowns of his back, culminating finally in a fusion operation, which were actually to lead this minister back to the simple, basic faith he had relinqushed many years before.

"One of the firmest tenets of my faith is that God never sends sickness upon His children," comments Dr. Rettig, "but I do know that God uses all the experiences of life, and can make them work out for good to them that love Him. It was when I was lying flat on my back, unable to move, that I learned to know Him as I never could have otherwise."

This clergyman had never believed in spiritual healing, but within a few weeks after his return to his pulpit, the evangelistic ministry of Kathryn Kuhlman was brought to his attention. Extremely skeptical, but curious, he attended one of her services and was amazed at what he saw.

"I wondered," he says, "why these 'signs and wonders' should not take place within our churches, where I felt they really belonged."

At just about that time Dr. Alfred Price came to Pittsburgh to conduct a healing mission at Trinity Episcopal Cathedral. Dr. Rettig attended these services and was profoundly impressed. After a long conference with Dr. Price, followed by some intensive research on the healing ministry, he started in his own church to preach on prayer and faith, praying for the sick, by name, before each Sunday sermon.

Remarkable healings began to occur with increasing frequency, and names for prayer poured in until they became too numerous to read. Dr. Rettig then established a Wednesday night prayer group, where names were read until the list again grew too long to permit individual mention.

In 1953 the clergyman procured permission from his Church Board to hold weekly healing services with the laying-on-of-hands. These services, held every Saturday afternoon, last one and one-half hours and are conducted quietly and reverently.

"I pray as the Holy Spirit guides me," explains Dr. Rettig, "and I have been told that the prayers are so appropriate to the condition of the individual that it seems as though I had known the need of each."

Two-thirds of the persons who attend these services are not members of St. Peter's, but represent many diverse denominations. Many come from great distances. To this congregation, the pastor continually emphasizes the primary purpose of spiritual healing, which is not, as he makes clear, the curing of the body, but rather, the healing of the spirit. Also, lest there be any misunderstanding, he impresses upon his people the fact that the healing ministry acknowledges the reality of sin, sickness, and suffering, and encourages the use of medical science. To make this point doubly clear, he has printed on the prayer request forms, "This is not a substitute for medical aid."

A monthly prayer letter with a revised sick list goes to hundreds of people in some thirty-six states. The vast majority of these have agreed to pray for the sick and for the healing ministry at St. Peter's. Many are the healings which occur under this ministry, both through intercessory prayer and as the result of direct contact: healings of alcoholism, mental sickness, and physical disease of all kinds. In virtually every instance a deep spiritual regeneration has taken place in the individual concerned.

Some cures are instantaneous. A woman suffering from blood poisoning, racked with chills and fever and in intense pain, attended a healing service en route to her doctor's. She was instantly and completely healed that afternoon at the church. A woman suffering acute pain from an internal hernia, went to St. Peter's a few days before her scheduled operation. During the prayer for the sick, she felt something like an electric current pour through her body. The pain increased almost beyond endurance (as is often the case in instantaneous healing) and then suddenly subsided. By the end of the service, she felt completely well. A visit to her doctor confirmed her expectation. "A perfect healing. No surgery required" was the verdict.

But Dr. Rettig points out that the majority of healings appear to be gradual. He cites, for example, the case of a man desperately ill with a grave heart condition. When the clergyman was called to the house, the patient's lungs had already filled with fluid (pulmonary edema). Diuretics had proved ineffective, and his condition was considered medically hopeless.

Before administering the healing rites, the Reverend Rettig talked at length to the man's wife, explaining to her the necessity, on her part, of what might perhaps be termed the ultimate in faith. "God has the last word," he explained. "There is nothing He cannot do. But He cannot accomplish His purpose until you learn to let go. You must be willing to commit your husband entirely to God, trusting Him implicitly."

This was far from easy for the apprehensive wife; but after much weeping and inner turmoil, she was able to say, and apparently mean: "God, he is Yours. Whatever You do is all right with me."

The clergyman then proceeded to the sickroom, and after praying with the patient, laid hands over his heart.

There was no immediately dramatic result, but within an amazingly short time thirteen quarts of fluid had drained from this man's body. He had lost thirty-one pounds in weight, and his blood pressure had dropped sixty-four points when he returned to his doctor. The physician shook his head, examined him again, then said: "I can't account for this thing, but you have a completely new machine inside you."

Richard Rettig frankly admits that he came close to intellectualizing himself out of faith. However, he discovered in time, and is now demonstrating for all to see, the dynamic power of practicing the full faith as opposed to the spiritual poverty which follows the equivocal belief of many modern intellectuals.

His former "erudite" and selective teaching, has been replaced by the preaching of an unadulterated Gospel, which points the way to holiness so simply that "wayfaring men, though fools, shall not err therein" (*Isaiah* 35:8).

This is a ministry of great spiritual power, founded on an arduously acquired child-like faith in the promises of Jesus Christ. It is an open channel for God's healing grace, as its leader bears eloquent witness to the eternal verity of Our Lord's Words: "If thou canst believe, all things are possible to him that believeth" (*Mark* 9:23).

CHAPTER 21

The Reverend Robert A. Russell

(*Episcopal*)

𝒞HE RECTOR of Denver's Epiphany Episcopal Church is a distinguished pioneer in the healing field.

It was more than twenty-five years ago, as a young minister just out of seminary, that Robert Russell took the healing ministry to the seven small mission churches in the mining camps of Colorado which he was then serving. Although spiritual healing was an entirely new concept to these mountain people, their response was overwhelming. The mountain chapels soon became too small to accommodate the crowds.

The young clergyman was then transferred to a small and moribund parish in Denver. This tiny church was destined to become, through its powerful ministry of healing, the second largest, the most dynamic and the most widely-publicized in Colorado.

In a matter of six months little Epiphany numbered among

its congregation and membership many of the richest, most influential, and prominent citizens of Colorado. Loud-speakers were installed in the crypt of the old building, but the crowds kept pressing upon the little structure until it became necessary to move the congregation to the South Gate Masonic Temple. Here, after only a few months, the same situation was repeated, and it was finally decided to build the present beautiful church which is also known as The Shrine of the Healing Presence.

Dr. Russell's unusually long interest in spiritual healing is understandable, for, as he explains: "Being blessed with a mother of great faith and spiritual power, and having seen so many miraculous answers to her prayers, it is only natural that I should have grown up believing that faith can accomplish anything."

One of his early contacts with the healing power of God, and one which made an indelible impression upon him, occurred when he was a small boy. It involved the instant healing of his mother from a strangulated hernia, in answer to prayer.

"That incident occurred fifty years ago," recalls the clergyman, "but I shall never forget the story as she told it to us children the next day. She said that as she prayed for healing, the Presence of Christ was so real and so near that she actually placed her hand in His."

In the early years of his healing work, before his ministry at Epiphany had assumed its present time-consuming proportions, Dr. Russell held healing missions in Episcopal churches all over the United States. One of the first of these was at La Jolla, California.

Here a devout Presbyterian woman, who had traveled eighty miles to attend the mission, was instantly healed of double cataracts. When she returned to the oculist next morning, he was amazed to find no evidence of the cataracts for which surgery had already been scheduled. This dramatic healing of a woman well known and highly respected in her community was instrumental in Dr. Russell's meteoric rise in the field of spiritual healing.

From the beginning of his healing ministry Dr. Russell has combined a metaphysical approach with emphasis on the Sacraments. The thousands to whom the Healing Shrine has successfully ministered vouch for the efficacy of his method.

Epiphany Church conducts two public healing services each week in the Shrine, both well attended by people of all denominations. At the Thursday morning service, divine healing is invoked for all on the prayer list, each name being mentioned aloud.

The evening service of the same day includes instructions by the rector and the laying-on-of-hands.

The prayer group which supports this ministry is known as the Silent Ministry of Healing. It comprises men and women especially trained in prayer who are devoting their lives to God's work for humanity.

"They are proving daily," says Dr. Russell, "that physical, financial, mental, and spiritual difficulties can be overcome by scientific prayer."

The clergyman makes clear, however, that the primary purpose of spiritual therapy is not to make unhappy people happy; or poor people rich; or sick people well.

"These are only results," he emphasizes. "The primary object is to help people realize the Presence of Christ."

He stresses the fact that healing lies in the total surrender of the individual to God.

"You must give Him your entire heart, mind, soul, and strength. In other words, you must 'put on the whole armour of God.' Only a part will not suffice."

To illustrate his meaning Dr. Russell cited the case of a devout woman who had asked him to pray for the healing of her broken hip which would not mend. In questioning the patient, the minister discovered that she was harboring a bitter resentment against the first doctor who had tended her injury; for he had set her hip incorrectly, with the result that it had to be re-set six months later by another physician.

In response to the woman's sincere assertion: "I believe that God can heal me," Dr. Russell replied: "Of course He can, but not until you give up this hatred which is generating poison in your mind."

"Well, there's nothing I can do about that," she answered, "for I shall hate that doctor as long as I live."

The clergyman left, unable to help her.

Several months later the woman again called him.

"I'm trying to love Dr. ———. Will you pray for me that I may be forgiven for the hatred I have been holding toward him?" she asked. She was subsequently quickly and completely healed, for she had "put on the *whole* armour of God," which in her case meant relinquishing her hatred and replacing it with love.

Dr. Russell is convinced that with absolute faith it is as easy to cure a cancer as a headache.

"Too often we open the mind through faith," he remarked, "and then slam it shut through doubt."

Not long ago, the clergyman was called to a hospital in the middle of the night. A seventy-year-old patient had fallen down a flight of stone steps, and for four days had lain in a coma with a fractured skull and other serious injuries.

Greeted at the hospital by a nurse and the patient's family, who had called him, Dr. Russell was told that three specialists had called the case hopeless. The woman was not expected to survive the night.

"Doubt and despair," says the minister, "are actually malignant forces operating against faith. They filled that hospital room. I asked the nurse to leave while I prayed, knowing that at a time like this, an unweakened and radical faith was needed; and that it was up to me to provide it."

Before the healing prayer was concluded, the patient had regained consciousness. The following day she went for a drive, and on the third day, went home from the hospital.

"Records of this sort are endless," commented Dr. Russell. "Undeviating faith invariably serves as the channel through which God moves."

The Reverend Robert Russell has dedicated his life to the restoration of the apostolic practice of healing in the Name of Jesus Christ by prayer, anointing, and the laying-on-of-hands. He has exerted a profound influence on the reestablishment of the identity of Christian healing with the whole Gospel of the Church Universal.

For many people in many churches, the name of this clergyman will be irrevocably linked with the twentieth-century revival of the great ministry of healing.

CHAPTER 22

The Reverends John A. Collins and Williston M. Ford

(Episcopal)

$\mathcal{G}$RACE EPISCOPAL CATHEDRAL in San Francisco was one of the first churches in the United States to institute the ministry of healing as we know it today. Here in 1920, as the result of an American mission held by the gifted English lay healer, James Moore Hickson, healing services were started by the Very Reverend J. Wilmer Gresham, Dean of the Cathedral. His distinguished ministry was to continue for over twenty years.

Participating in the early development of the Cathedral's Mission of Healing were two young clergymen, John Collins and Williston Ford. They were to assist the Dean for some years until, transferred from the Cathedral to different parishes, they went their separate ways, each taking to whatever church he served the ministry of healing.

By strange coincidence these two ministers, whose experience in the healing field has run so curiously parallel (both are now chaplains of the Order of St. Luke), have found themselves reunited at St. Peter's-by-the-Golden Gate. Here the Reverend Collins, as rector of this church, is conducting an effective healing ministry, aided and supported by his colleague, Williston Ford, who, although retired from the active ministry, continues his healing work as chaplain of the St. Luke Mission.

History has seemed to repeat itself for these two clergymen at St. Peter's. For as their efforts were instrumental in bringing healing to the San Francisco area through the Cathedral, so have they again restored this ministry to the community through their present church, which has replaced the healing services at the Cathedral, discontinued after Dean Gresham's retirement.

It was in 1949 that the Reverend Collins instituted his weekly healing services at St. Peter's after the congregation's interest had been sparked by visits from the Reverend John Gaynor Banks and Bishop Austin Pardue.

"From their inception," says Mr. Collins, "these services have attracted many people from faraway places." In fact, so widespread has been the interest and so urgent the demand, that it has been hoped that the healing ministry would soon be revived in Grace Cathedral. In view of the sentiments of Dean James A. Pike, newly elected Bishop Coadjutor of the Diocese of California, there is good reason to believe that this hope will be realized. Dean Pike made very clear to me his stand on spiritual healing when he recently said: "I am of course interested in and sympathetic to the revival and advance of the ministry of healing as any priest of our Church should be."

Meanwhile Mr. Collins has patterned his healing service after that used by Dean Gresham in the Cathedral.

The Tuesday evening gathering starts as a prayer group, remembering the names of those who ask help. Then follow the hymns and an address which immediately precedes the laying-on-of-hands. This rite is performed as though Christ were speaking through the ministrant, whose hands release His healing power.

The atmosphere of the service induces a very real sense of the Presence of Our Lord, "thought of as the Presence of Love," says Mr. Ford. "Christ being the eternal manifestation of love, His power presides and prevails in a very natural yet marvelous way."

Father Ford, in citing his own peace of soul and nervous rehabilitation which has resulted from his knowledge of the healing Christ, mentions the power of what he calls "spiritual relaxation" in a childbirth case of a few weeks ago.

The tense, frightened young mother went to the clergyman for help. After praying with her he gave her a simple meditation based on the words, "Be still and know that I am Love."

When the young woman arrived at the hospital, she appeared so tranquil that one of the nurses told her to return home until her labor had properly begun. The patient, however, insisted on examination; whereupon it was discovered that she was in the final stage of labor. Delivery was quick, and her recovery unusually rapid.

Through his healing ministry over the years, the Reverend Ford has continually emphasized that love heals; that God's infinite Love is the Healer; and that God above, dwelling within, is the focal or contact point of healing.

"Recognition of this truth," he says, "raises spiritual healing far above the level of magic or wishful thinking." This recognition, fostered by the healing ministry, results in many transformed lives, as was the case of a woman who had been under a doctor's care for several years, for a number of valid physical ailments. Physically sick, nervously exhausted, and mentally depressed over her long invalidism, the ministry of healing was finally brought to her attention by a solicitous friend. Skeptical, she nevertheless agreed to do some reading on that subject and attend a few healing services. Almost despite herself, she gradually became aware of the reality of the living Christ, who by His love heals all who turn to him. In a remarkably short time this woman was completely healed. Today, filled with gratitude and the love of God, she is radiant with a happiness which infects all those who come in contact with her.

"While we do not keep case records," says Mr. Collins, "there are continued witnessings given of healing."

In view of the number of cancer cases which have come to his attention, where resentment and hostility were invariably evident in the patient, Father Ford has become a firm advocate of the medical school of thought which is coming to believe that all disease may actually be psychosomatic or the result of stress.

He cites as a typical example the case of a forty-five-year old woman who was suffering from a large uterine growth. In talking to this patient, Mr. Ford discovered that she was harboring an overwhelming resentment against her husband because of his conjugal demands upon her. Through counseling and healing prayer, this patient was finally able to overcome her feelings of hostility and resentment. A short time after she had happily assumed her marital responsibility, she returned to the doctor for examination. There was no evidence whatsoever of the former growth.

Both Mr. Collins and Mr. Ford, as a result of their long experience in the healing field, are convinced that teaching and healing should go hand in hand. They recall the cessation of healing services at Grace Cathedral when Dean Gresham retired, and agree that "People had relied so much upon the loving personality of the Dean that his absence resulted in a gradual loss of expectancy. Unless teaching is made inseparable from healing, people tend to depend upon the power of a personality rather than on God."

They emphasize also that to "guarantee" healing or to anoint with consecrated oil without teaching the purpose of spiritual healing is dangerous and bound to end in disappointment, even though a temporary physical benefit may result.

"Without a prayer group," says Mr. Ford, "and without teaching, healing is able to rest only upon blind faith, self-persuasion, egocentric reliance upon one's own will, dependence upon some leader's personality, or passive credulity. None of these impart permanent cure or spiritual rebirth."

Participants in the healing ministry of St. Peter's-by-the Golden Gate are conscious of the fact that, since Love is the Life of God, His Nature and His Being, each instant of Love heals. Touched by the Holy Spirit at work in this church, its members have come into a new awareness of a great truth: that Jesus Christ resides within each awakened soul.

CHAPTER 23

Agnes Sanford

(*Lay Healer*)

I VENTURE to say that there is no member of the laity in the United States who is wielding a greater or more widespread influence on the revival of healing within the churches than Agnes Sanford, daughter of a Presbyterian missionary and wife of an Episcopal priest.

Her first book, *The Healing Light,* published in 1947, has gone into nineteen editions and has been reprinted in seven languages. Not only has it guided innumerable laymen into a knowledge of the healing Christ, but it has served as both a revelation and a text book for hundreds of clergymen of all denominations.

Its author is a small woman of immense spiritual stature, vibrant with the love and vitality of God. A realist with a dash of mysticism, she is a curious combination of creative imagination and objective rationalism; of intellectuality and childish simplicity; of deep religiosity, yet with something of the scientist's dedication to the principle that the fundamental laws of the universe cannot be broken.

"The scientist," she writes "has faith in the laws of nature, combined with perfect humility towards these laws, and a patient determination to learn them at whatever cost. Through this humility, scientists have learned how to conform to the laws of nature, and by so doing have achieved results. Through the same meekness, those who seek God can produce results by learning to conform to His laws of faith and love."

Convinced that God does nothing except by law, Mrs. Sanford is equally convinced that He has provided enough power within His law to do anything that is in accordance with His will. Confident that His will is for health, and that within man's body are vital forces that make for health when God's love is channeled into him through faith, Mrs. Sanford's concern is that a patient's mind and body be open to the goodness and love of God. As she makes clear, "the infinite and eternal life of God cannot help us unless we are prepared to receive that life within ourselves."

It was twenty-five years ago that Agnes Sanford had her first experience with God's healing power. Her infant son had been ill for over six weeks with abscessed ears. As her prayers for his healing appeared unanswered, her bitterness and doubt grew. Then one afternoon a young minister stopped by the Sanford's home. Immediately on hearing of the baby's illness, he said: "I'll go up and have a prayer with him." Walking over to the crib, he placed his hands on the child's ears, and said a simple prayer, ending with a spontaneous word of faith: "Now shut your eyes and go to sleep, and when you wake up you will be all right." Instantly the baby fell asleep; he woke up the next morning completely well.

"This incident," says Mrs. Sanford, "turned on the light for me. It showed me that God is an active and powerful reality."

A year later, suffering from profound depression, she sought out this same clergyman and asked his prayers. He laid his hands on her head, and prayed for the healing of her mind and nerves. "No problems were solved," recalls Mrs. Sanford, "because neither he nor I knew what they were. But I was marvelously healed. From that time forward, I began to learn. I followed this young minister's suggestions for prayer, and slowly the faith that I had said in words, unbelieving, came to me.

"I then asked him whether he thought a layman could learn to help people as he had helped me. He answered yes, and prayed for me to receive the gift of healing."

After a few experiments with prayer Agnes Sanford began to realize it was God's will that she enter the then virtually uncharted sea of spiritual healing. After a year of Bible study, "to see exactly what the Word taught about this matter," she began her work. "I knew," she says, "that I must go about this thing slowly; and I learned by doing."

It soon became evident that the young clergyman's prayer in her behalf had been answered, for she possessed an undeniable charismatic gift of healing, which has grown to an extraordinary degree over the years—a fact that causes her to believe that anyone with a sincere desire to heal can cultivate this gift by prayer and spiritual discipline.

By lecturing, writing, and conducting healing missions throughout the nation, many in conjunction with her clergyman husband, she has spread the word of the healing Christ. She works interdenominationally, but always within the framework of the organized Church. Clergymen of all denominations have come to accept the theological integrity of her teaching, as well as the evidence of the healing power of God which her work so thrillingly demonstrates.

Take, for example, the case of a small child dying of a brain tumor, who was brought to her for prayer and the laying-on-of-hands. The medical prognosis was total blindness within a few weeks, followed rapidly by death. The little girl

was taken to Mrs. Sanford by her parents and their Presbyterian minister, who knew virtually nothing of spiritual healing. What he learned that afternoon was to re-vitalize his ministry. The child received healing from Mrs. Sanford and today
appears well.

Or take the case of the man with a badly damaged heart,
who was instantly healed by God's power after he received
the laying-on-of-hands. Or the instant healing of a pneumonia case. Or the healing within a week of a woman whose
physical health was shattered, and whom psychiatrists had
given up—a woman so seriously disturbed emotionally that she
had made two suicide attempts.

The tremendously large number of remarkable healings of
this sort which have taken place under Mrs. Sanford's lay
ministry are well known. She is so constantly in demand to
pray with and for the sick that it has been difficult for her to
concentrate on what, from the beginning, has been her aim
and purpose: to teach people to pray and heal so that the
ministry of healing may be restored to its rightful place in
the whole church.

Two years ago the way to do just this opened up for her. A
teaching center for spiritual healing was established in Whit-
insville, Massachusetts. She and her husband head this School
of Pastoral Care. Sponsored by eminent clergymen of many
denominations and by a number of doctors and psychiatrists,
their school is, as Mrs. Sanford puts it, "for the purpose of
passing on to clergymen of all churches what we have learned
of faith and prayer. Our aim is to help ministers to a better
understanding of how they can aid their people in illness,
depression, alcoholism, emotional disturbances, and guilt
complexes."

Mrs. Sanford explains that the sessions held at the school
are not retreats or conferences, but classes held to instruct the
clergy in intercessions and the laying-on-of-hands; to lead
them to a deeped realization of the spiritual power that is

the heritage of all Christian ministers—the same power practiced by the apostles.

The response to the school has been extremely gratifying. At the request of many clergymen, its activities were recently expanded to include sessions for their wives as well as themselves; and, at the request of the Right Reverend William Lawrence, Episcopal Bishop of Western Massachusetts, at least one session each summer is to be held for lay people. But these lay sessions are strictly "extras." The emphasis and real purpose of the school is on and for clerical instruction.

Through this teaching center the healing ministry is being spread through the churches of America in a way not possible by any other means. Already the healing work of its "graduates" is becoming known. They come from as far south as Florida and Texas, as far north as the outposts of Canada and Alaska; they include Episcopalians, Methodists, Presbyterians, Lutherans, Congregationalists, Baptists, and others.

"Here we work together," says Mrs. Sanford, "in fellowship and unity in the world of prayer, where no compromise is necessary."

The contribution of Agnes Sanford to the healing ministry is two-fold: as a remarkable conductor of God's love, she fully demonstrates His healing power. As an outstanding teacher of His spiritual laws, she is handing on, so that it may perpetually flame within the Church, the torch lit by her conviction of the Kingdom which is within us all.

CHAPTER 24

Louise W. Eggleston

(*Lay Healer*)

$\mathcal{S}$OME years ago Louise Eggleston, outstanding Methodist churchwoman, learned of the healing power of God released through prayer. Since that time, as founder and leader of the interdenominational World Literacy Prayer Group which meets at Ghent Methodist Church in Norfolk, Virginia, and as Spiritual Life Leader of the Virginia Conference of Methodist Women, Mrs. Eggleston has devoted her life to sharing her knowledge with others. Through her pamphlets on prayer, her work in churches all over the nation, and her activity and leadership in Christian Camp work, she has made, and continues to make, an outstanding contribution to the cause of spiritual healing.

In all her work, although it is interdenominational, she keeps the Church central; for she says: "All I have I've been given through the Church. I believe that it is the Body of Christ made visible on earth."

Mrs. Eggleston speaks with authority on spiritual healing, for she herself has twice been remarkably healed by God's power.

Her first healing occurred at the age of eight. When she was away from home on a visit to the country, she was seized with severe abdominal pains. When the home remedies of her hostess failed to alleviate the pain and fever, a country doctor was called in. He was unable to diagnose her case, but recognized her condition as critical, and urged her immediate return home while she was still living. Her parents were notified to meet the child with the best doctors in Norfolk. Two surgeons and the family physician made the diagnosis: ruptured appendix, peritonitis, with one chance in a thousand of surviving surgery.

The family doctor vouchsafed his opinion: "She will never come through surgery alive. My best advice is to commit her to the Great Physician for healing. He is the only One who can do it."

Her father, a Methodist clergyman, and her mother finally agreed. The parents and this Christian doctor met and prayed together for the small girl's life. She was marvelously healed.

From the time she became a teen-aged girl Louise Eggleston tried to follow the teachings of her parents, who constantly reminded her that God had saved her for a purpose.

"I considered myself a very good Christian," she recalls now, with a smile. "I never stayed away from Sunday school or church if it were possible for me to go. I even taught Sunday school. In fact, I did everything I was asked, except join a new prayer group. My excuse was that I was too busy to attend another meeting. The truth was that going to a prayer group meeting didn't sound nearly so alluring as the garden club or a bridge game."

Then at the age of forty Mrs. Eggleston became critically ill for the second time in her life. She had been in pain for some time before she sought medical advice. When she finally consulted her doctor, she was told that she had waited too long. Surgery, he said, would be useless, for the obviously malignant growth had metastasized. Finally at her family's insistence, the doctor reluctantly agreed to undertake what he considered a hopeless operation.

The little prayer group that Louise Eggleston had refused to join, prayed for her throughout the operation. When at the end the surgeon said she was still breathing but could not survive owing to the extensive damage of vital organs, the group continued to pray. Their faith was rewarded by the patient's complete recovery.

"So humbled was I by the Christ-like spirit of this little group," says Mrs. Eggleston, "that I promised my Saviour my life should belong to Him completely."

She has kept her promise, and has let God do with her as He wills. "Spiritual adventuring with the Lord," she says, "is the most thrilling experience one can ever know."

Mrs. Eggleston has done a great deal of research in prayer, and is by now wholly convinced that prayer has never caused God to change His will or break His spiritual laws. "Prayer," says Louise Eggleston, "changes *us* and makes us one with His will, His way, and His law. It is through our oneness with Him that we make contact with the Power that controls the universe."

She emphasizes continually that the primary aim in her life service is not physical healing, but the healing of the soul. Convinced that all disease begins in the soul, mind, and personality of men, and that no body can be permanently cured unless it is healed at the source of the disease, she refers to herself as a "soul surgeon."

"I know beyond the shadow of any doubt," she says, "that when we get the soul and mind in harmony with the will of God and His plan for our lives, the body will be made 'every whit whole,' regardless of its present condition."

Healing, in the opinion of Louise Eggleston, is like joy or

goodness or success—a highway over which we travel to reach a higher goal, that of healing the soul.

She points out that Jesus met people at the place of their need, and used their awareness of some human need to reveal to them a deeper need. And so it is today that she ministers to human needs in order that the deeper need may be met.

When she prays with a person for healing, she always lays hands on him in order "to be God's contact," as she expresses it. Unless she is asked, she does not tell patients why she does this; but she has found that this method of prayer brings a better response in the one seeking help.

She often gives the sick one a promise of Jesus to hold, saying: "You are holding onto a promise that Jesus gave us all. It is the Word of God upon which our entire universe is founded. It cannot fail, but you must notice that His promises always carry conditions. You must meet these conditions, for God is bound by His Own Laws."

Louise Eggleston can cite many wonderful manifestations of the healing power of God which have resulted from prayer.

A woman, for example, was dying of leukemia. A group of her friends met at the altar for prayer, meditation, and Holy Communion. An immediate improvement was noted in the patient's condition. She improved steadily, and her healing was a source of wonder and delight to both doctors and friends.

A woman suffered from tuberculosis of the spine; three inches in the middle of the spine had been destroyed, and three inches of the lower extremity. For a number of weeks devout friends prayed fervently for her recovery. One day she suddenly felt a warm glow pass up her spine. She cried, "I am well," and leaped to her feet. She could walk, and the healing was from that moment complete and permanent. Her doctor took her before a New York association, and said: "Before this happened I was an atheist. Now I am a Christian."

A child was operated on for a brain tumor. Throughout the ordeal of surgery, the child was surrounded and upheld by group prayer. She made a speedy and uneventful recovery. It was not until months later that Mrs. Eggleston learned from the operating surgeon that when the incision was made and the child's condition fully revealed, he knew she was wholly beyond medical help. As the child was obviously expiring on the operating table, the surgeons waited briefly before closing the wound, intending to perform a post mortem. They were incredulous as suddenly the child's pulse grew discernibly stronger, her breathing more regular. Conscious of a "strange sort of healing Presence" which seemed to envelop them all, the doctors closed the incision, having performed no surgery of any kind. The child's recovery was rapid and complete. Today, years later, she is in radiant health.

Mrs. Eggleston feels that the many healings of this sort which have occurred are the result of yielding to God, of allowing Him to do what He has been waiting for a chance to do.

"Let Him have you," she says, "so that He may heal you. For always remember that the price of spiritual power is unconditional surrender to God."

Louise Eggleston is herself a living testimony to the validity of her words.

CHAPTER 25

Oral Roberts

(*Evangelist*)

Many of us are by now familiar with the background of Oral Roberts, the thirty-nine-year-old revivalist—of how, three months before his birth, this son of a Pentecostal minister was dedicated to God by his mother; how, at the age of sixteen, a stutterer and long bed-ridden with tuberculosis, the frail boy saw a vision of Christ while he and his father prayed together, and so strong was the Presence that Oral rose from his bed, crying: "I am saved!"; how, five months later, the boy was taken to a revivalist healing service and heard the Voice of God say to him: "Son, I am going to heal you, and you are going to take my healing power to your generation"; how, completely healed that night of both his stammering and tuberculosis, young Oral began preaching some two months afterward; and how, twelve years later, while serving as the ordained minister of a Pentecostal Holiness Church, the

Reverend Roberts received through fasting and prayer the revelation from God he had long been awaiting.

The evangelist will undoubtedly remain a controversial figure for as long as he continues to command such a tremendous audience; but I have observed with interest that as public knowledge of spiritual healing has grown, hostility toward the Roberts' ministry has diminished. Those who know most of the healing ministry, the healing clergy of the established Church, tend to be the most tolerant of the evangelist's work. They recognize the validity of his premises, even though they cannot accept his technique.

Episcopal Bishop Austin Pardue, for example, says: "While I couldn't possibly work as does Mr. Roberts, and temperamentally dislike his methods, I definitely *like* the fact that he is helping so many. There are great masses of people who seem to need such a ministry. Oral Roberts and others like him are reaching people their critics will never reach. I think it's presumptuous to blindly condemn and ridicule anyone working in Christ's Name. 'Judge not that ye be not judged' is something it behooves all of us to remember."

Several months ago the evangelist was invited to come to New York to participate in a seminar on spiritual healing with a number of eminent clergymen of conservative churches. Methodist minister Harry Robinson, Jr., voiced the opinion of most of those present, when he said: "Although I have some reservations about Mr. Roberts' manner, I nevertheless believe that he is a completely, sincerely dedicated man. There is no doubt of the many healings which occur under his ministry, and I am particularly impressed with his work among special groups, such as the American Indians, and his no-receipts missionary trips abroad each year. Furthermore his personal receipts seem so hedged about that they cannot become inordinately large, so he is not plagued with self-interest. He is serving sacrificially."

In his essential teaching Mr. Roberts actually hews closely

to the line held by the traditional Church in its ministry of spiritual healing. His emphasis is continually on the soul's salvation, not the body's healing.

"I believe that physical health is the will of God," the evangelist states, "but I have no interest in healing apart from salvation. My concern is with the saving of souls, which is the greatest of all miracles."

This is the underlying theme of his ministry, evidenced by his preaching, and carried out in the format of his services, wherein he never prays for the sick until he has attempted to lead people to Christ. Convinced that "Faith cometh by hearing the Word of God," Mr. Roberts preaches his sermon first. He immediately follows it with a plea that those who accept Jesus renounce their sins and come forward. Only then does he offer prayers for the sick.

Healings of virtually every known ailment—congenital, organic, and functional—have been claimed under the Roberts ministry. The evangelist refuses to hazard a guess as to what percentage are healed; and no attempt has been made to estimate the number of genuine healings which occur, as opposed to the inevitable false claims.

A substantial number of healings brought to my attention are obviously of a psychotherapeutic nature. However, many claimed healings of both organic physical and mental disease appear entirely valid on the basis of the original medical diagnosis and the patient's apparently robust health several years later. That these dramatic physical healings appear to be accompanied by powerful spiritual regeneration would seem to remove the Roberts' ministry from any suspicion of charlatanism.

The case of Henry Holt, president of the New York textile firm which bears his name, is typical of many.

Supposedly dying of cancer four years ago, Holt was, as he puts it, "nagged into attending a Roberts campaign by my wife. A hard-headed business man and a skeptic, I was convinced the whole thing was a gigantic fraud. But I was just too weak to resist, so like a drowning man grasping at a straw, I had my handy man drive me down."

By the time Mr. Holt got in the healing line, after first being "saved," and then, in a smaller tent, praying for forgiveness for his sins, he was even more convinced than he had been in the beginning that the thing was a fake.

"And as soon as my turn came up to be 'healed,'" he said, "I intended to tell Mr. Roberts exactly what I thought of him in front of the audience.

Preceding me in line was a club-footed boy who was seemingly healed. Then directly in front of me was a Methodist minister from Los Angeles whose wife, standing beside him, had a large goiter on her neck. I remember thinking, 'This I got to see.'

"At that moment Oral Roberts started calling on the Lord to heal that woman. All of a sudden she gulped, and to my amazement the goiter disappeared. I was absolutely stupefied —and in that instant my whole slant on life seemed to change. When it was my turn to face Mr. Roberts, I was still so stunned I couldn't answer him intelligently. My prepared speech excoriating him was forgotten. I vaguely remember him praying for me—and my surprise when I realized I was praying with him.

"After the prayers were over, I felt a tremor go through my system. A feeling of exultation seemed to wash over me, bringing with it a feeling of complete peace of mind and body which seemed to eliminate all my problems. I walked down the ramp, still dazed, but with a lightness in my soul it is impossible to describe."

Henry Holt claims that he was healed that night. Virtually bankrupt by the expenses of his illness, since regaining his health, he has worked hard to put his business back on its feet. "With the help of God, I am succeeding," he says.

As a consequence of his healing, he has regained all his long-lost religious beliefs. He and his wife have become faithful churchgoers, and powerful witnesses for the healing Christ.

"I'm not the emotional type," the business man assured me. "But I love my Saviour and will always testify to His almighty greatness. Mr. Roberts did not heal me, but he led me to the God who did. I shall always be grateful to him."

The Roberts' organization, manned by three hundred and fifty workers, receives, in addition to 150,000 letters a month, some 5,000 testimonies of claimed healings every week. These are carefully screened, and those which appear in his magazine, *Abundant Life,* are first investigated by a committee. If there is any doubt as to the authenticity of a healing, the account is not printed. "Of course we're not infallible," remarked the evangelist, "and we've made mistakes. But we do all in our power to reduce such mistakes to a minimum. We wait at least a year, and preferably two, before publicly acknowledging a healing."

Faced with the problem of all evangelists of becoming a "cult," Mr. Roberts takes every precaution to avert this. Although frequently asked to start a Bible school and send out missionaries, he adamantly refuses.

"As you well know," he said to me, "This is not a new 'movement.' I am simply preaching the Gospel of Jesus Christ —and I will work only through existing churches."

As a result of this policy many orthodox churchmen are losing their antipathy toward the evangelist. They see and acknowledge the results of his revival in their own churches.

"I can't do a pastor's job," explains Mr. Roberts, "I simply haven't time. My task, my method, was given me by God, and I work as I have been directed. We are the shock troops to attract sinners, and bring them to God. It is up to the individual pastor to do the follow-up job."

The evangelist obviously has time during a meeting personally to lay hands on only a small percentage of those who seek healing. Healings, however, are by no means restricted to those he physically touches. Like the small, hunch-backed woman sitting in the last row during a recent crusade, whose back grew straight and strong as Mr. Roberts prayed for the sick, healings occur throughout the tent or auditorium.

"There is no healing power in my hands," Oral Roberts insists. "They are only points of contact."

Yet there is no gainsaying the clearly discernible current of power transmitted through these hands. Despite this fact, the evangelist vehemently denies the possession of a charismatic gift of healing. Only under some pressure will he acknowledge that he is a uniquely open channel for the healing power.

"If I had any choice in the matter," says Mr. Roberts, "I would choose the gift of wisdom. Whatever 'gift' I may seem to have now, it is not a twenty-four hour affair. It comes only with anointing, when the Holy Spirit is upon me. That happens most often when I am preaching. Even if I had time, I could not work privately with the sick. I just can't turn to healing at any moment of the day. As I preach I become more and more aware of the Presence of Christ, until finally the spirit of God takes possession of me—and using me, allows me to do things I could not normally do, of myself."

How many of the millions of souls saved under his guidance will remain "saved," no one knows. However, Oral Roberts' work is a dramatic demonstration that the healing ministry is the most powerful instrument of conversion the world has yet known. I suggest that an unprecedentedly large number of these conversions will last; for those who have visibly witnessed and tangibly felt the Holy Spirit do not easily forget the experience.

A man with a very great healing ministry within the Church, Dr. Alfred Price, says: "I feel that Oral Roberts is being used by God mightily."

Oral Roberts is what he claims to be: a simple man who

loves Jesus; a man who is devoting his life to preaching the love and compassion of God, at the same time recognizing that the Presence of the Holy Spirit is a Presence of Judgment as well as of Grace.

26

Kathryn Kuhlman

(*Evangelist*)

$\mathcal{F}$ROM the beginning of her evangelistic career, the mission of Kathryn Kuhlman has been "to help those who are hungry for Christ to find Him"; and from the beginning, the theme of all her sermons has been faith.

It was twelve years ago, in Franklin, Pennsylvania, that members of her congregation suddenly began to claim spontaneous healings during her services. As the number of these healings increased, the Baptist-ordained minister began to preach on healing through faith. Thus began today's "miracle" services.

In 1948 she settled in Pittsburgh, and established the schedule to which she still adheres: two weekly services in Pittsburgh; one in Youngstown, Ohio; and every third week, a service in Cleveland.

Under this ministry I have seen tumors dissolve; the blind see; the deaf hear; and the crippled walk. In none of these cases have I trusted my own vision, but have had scores of such healings medically verified.

To the frequent charge that such cures are hysterical and not permanent, Kathryn Kuhlman replies: "Those whom God heals stay healed." As many of the cases I have checked date from as long as twelve years ago, this statement would seem essentially true.

The answer to the charge that hypnotism or mass psychology is involved in these cures lies in the multitudinous healings which occur as the result of prayer requests and not personal attendance at the Kuhlman meetings.

One of many such cases is that of Mrs. Stella Turner, wife of an Internal Revenue worker in western Pennsylvania. She was operated on in 1952, supposedly for the removal of her gall bladder. When her abdomen was incised, the surgeon discovered that she had cancer of the gall bladder, liver, stomach, bowels, and pancreas. This diagnosis was confirmed by five attending physicians, who agreed that surgery was impossible and the patient's condition hopeless. Nine days later she was sent home from the hospital, in intense pain, to die.

A prayer request was sent in to Kathryn Kuhlman, written by the patient's sister and mailed by her husband at three A.M.

The following day the patient began what appeared to be pernicious vomiting. At the end of thirty-six hours she was without pain and confident that she had been healed. A subsequent check by her doctor confirmed the cure. "Five of us were not wrong," he said. "You have been healed by faith."

Mrs. Turner is today in perfect health. Both she and her husband are living dedicated lives in gratitude to God. Could this healing, and the numerous others like it, be attributed to either mass psychology or hypnosis?

But Kathryn Kuhlman's primary interest is in bringing souls to God; and, dramatic and awe-inspiring as are the cures of the body under this ministry, even more impressive are the healings of the spirit: the alcoholics, instantly healed, who have made Christ, not alcohol, the center of their lives; the drug addicts, miraculously cured, who live no longer for heroin, but for God; and the thousands of ordinary people like you and me, whose radiant faces and transformed lives reflect the God they have found under Miss Kuhlman's guidance.

The influence of this evangelist extends beyond the thousands of her personal followers and her two million radio listeners into many of the orthodox churches, for a substantial number of curious clergymen have attended her services and have been impressed. Her continual plea to "Start a healing ministry in *your* church; for every clergyman can and should have such a ministry," has not fallen on deaf ears. Some of the area's most effective church healing ministries have been instituted as a direct result of her inspiration. Furthermore, her insistence that her followers attend their own churches has resulted in a powerful spiritual revival in many community churches. As one clergyman confided to me: "Among my parishioners are many whose whole lives have been changed by the inspired faith of Kathryn Kuhlman. Now they never miss a Sunday, and have revitalized this church by their establishment of powerful prayer groups."

The fact that Miss Kuhlman has remained in one location for ten years and that her ministry has successfully survived the criticism which is the lot of all evangelists, is a tribute to her integrity. When asked why she does not extend the scope of her influence by traveling, her reply is: "My purpose is to save souls, and my particular calling is to offer proof of the power of God. I feel I can accomplish this more effectively by staying in one place where I am in a position to follow through on my people, and to insist that those who claim healings procure medical verification."

This emphasis on medical verification has done much to reduce the false claims of healing and the fanaticism which are inevitably associated with evangelistic healing. Insistence on scientific substantiation has not only contributed to the soundness of her personal ministry but to spiritual healing everywhere.

But if there are advantages to remaining in one location, there are also hazards; chief among them the overwhelming danger, in even so gifted a ministry as Kathryn Kuhlman's, that the instrument of His power, a blonde, slender evangelist, shall be mistaken by her devoted followers for the Source; that Kathryn Kuhlman may be worshiped rather than the Lord she represents. Of this peril the evangelist is well aware, and wages a constant battle to avert it. "I of myself am nothing," she repeats again and again. "It is the power of God, released by your faith, which heals you."

"My constant, overriding fear," she said to me, "is that I may grieve the Holy Spirit. No one knows better than I that without Him I am nothing, and have nothing."

I believe it is the genuineness of this fear which has thus far safeguarded her ministry from corruption or abuse.

The Reverend Gaius Slosser, D.D., eminent Presbyterian theologian, says: "Through the centuries there have occasionally appeared outstanding geniuses in the field of the spirit. Kathryn Kuhlman is one of these."

Many may, of course, continue to deplore Kathryn Kuhlman's evangelistic methods. For it is true that although, compared to many revivalist meetings, the Kuhlman services are decorous and well-controlled, compared to the traditional church, they are highly emotional. Yet dare we, who may prefer the orthodox church, disdain as "undignified" a method so abundantly endowed with the Presence of the Holy Spirit? Dare we who may believe in the sacramental approach disparage as "sensational" any service which is made so by the power of the living God?

The Reverend Owen Walton, Methodist minister and former executive secretary of the Council of Churches of Allegheny County, Pennsylvania, says: "Kathryn Kuhlman is undoubtedly bringing hope and faith to many thousands whom the established churches are not reaching at all."

The implication in this statement seems clear. When these established churches have universally revived the healing ministry within their own bodies, many of their people who are starving now for demonstrable evidence of the living God will no longer need to seek this evidence in tents and auditoriums. Meanwhile, for those thousands who have sought Him in vain at the altars of their own churches, Kathryn Kuhlman is pointing the way. She is providing the lamp that they may find His Kingdom in their hearts.

CHAPTER 27

The Great Reconciler

THROUGH the healing ministry of the Christian churches, the Universal Church is meeting with the most conspicuous success, the greatest challenge in her long history. Through this ministry we see most clearly demonstrated the transforming power of the Christian faith. The healing Church offers us unimpeachable evidence that with the resurgence of the traditional faith there is a corresponding and unmistakable renewal of the Holy Spirit.

Events have proved that the layman wants, and has the capacity to receive, an anchoring, definitive faith. He no longer shuns religion because it is too difficult, or the wages of sin too high. He does not feel the miraculous truths of Christianity to be intellectually incompatible. He believes in the full use of his God-given mind and in the ceaseless pursuit of knowledge; but he has learned that a philosophy is a poor substitute for faith. In a perhaps instinctive recoil against the heresy of gnosticism, he has realized that the Kingdom of Heaven cannot be attained by the intellect alone; nor can knowledge, of itself, save souls.

"By their fruits ye shall know them." That there is power in the historic Church is not a matter of idle conjecture. We see its dramatic and incontestable demonstration in the healing Church. To the exact extent that the Church fulfils Our Lord's Commission, believing and acting upon His promises, so is the limitless power of the Holy Spirit being unmistakably manifested today.

As a result of his observation of the healing ministry at work, the modernist is beginning to re-define the word Christian. He is recognizing that it involves more than adherence to an ethical code; more than a vague, generalized belief in the "Fatherhood of God and brotherhood of man" precept. He is discovering that mental approbation of a Palestinian reformer's teaching cannot replace the heart's acceptance of the Man Himself. He sees operating in the healing church the unique power of the Risen Christ, the result of an unattenuated Christian faith. On the one hand is today's self-serving religion which conceives of God as a flunkey whose duty it is to serve us health and happiness on a silver platter; on the other, yesterday's concept of Him, who with unthinkable cruelty saw fit to afflict us with unbearable suffering and disease "for our own good." The seeking layman has come at last to rest between the two extremes in the healing Church. If the Church is rediscovering the boundless power of the Holy Spirit, so through exposure to this ministry, is the individual Christian becoming once again an unmistakable exponent of his faith. He has put on the "armour of light" of which St. Paul speaks. Regardless of whether or not he has been physically cured, he has been transfigured by the touch of the healing Christ.

The ministry of spiritual healing is proving itself to be one of the strongest of all religious ties which bind together churches everywhere. Doctrinal differences tend to be forgotten, and dogmatic dissimilarities overlooked. The only essential tenet becomes a universal awareness of the recreating power of the living God, through His Son, Our Lord.

The Reverend Dixon Rollit, an Episcopal priest who is frequently called upon to minister to members of other denominations, cites a typical experience. "Just last week, for example," he reports, "I visited a four-bed ward in a large city hospital. In one bed lay the Methodist who had requested that I come to lay-on-hands. In the other three beds lay, respectively, a Lutheran, a Baptist, and a Roman Catholic. With bowed heads they all joined in the healing prayer. The following day all four patients showed what the doctors called a 'remarkable and unpredicted improvement.' "

While the healing ministry is only one of the many ministries of the Church, it is a fusion of them all. It is the catalyst which ignites the flame of faith that illuminates the whole Church and charges it with dynamic power. It is the ministry which is serving to unify the Christian world. For it is the unity of faith in the will and power of God to heal which is inspiring the sort of interdenominational teamwork manifested in one representative community during last Lenten season. Here the midweekly Lutheran Vespers service was conducted in a Methodist Church, attended by a large Presbyterian congregation, while an Episcopal minister preached and laid hands on those who desired healing. Side by side, not in stultifying uniformity, but in concord and unity of faith, we see here in action the Universal Church sharing the common prayer that it may be "delivered from all false doctrine, heresy, and schism"; jointly petitioning that it shall be "illuminated with true knowledge and understanding of His Word" (*Book of Common Prayer*).

It is in the Church Universal that the complete answer to spiritual healing must be found, as it is in the undivided Church that the full power and dazzling glory of Christianity will eventually be realized.

Healing is the ministry of great reconciliation, by which thousands have come closer to Jesus and are living redeemed lives in His Name. Through this ministry we glimpse a Christian Church, united by an unshakable faith in the totality of Our Lord's redemptive mission; an impregnable fortress, inviolable by reason of its foundation of immutable truth, against which the antichrist must hurl itself in vain.

Through Baptism and Holy Communion the Church offers us the means of spiritual regeneration. Through the preaching of God's Word it points the way to the Kingdom. Through the healing ministry, we enter in.

This is not to say that spiritual healing is the only way in which the Holy Spirit operates; or that it is the only road to belief in God. But for those of us who have for so long "looked through a glass darkly," seeing, no matter how we strained our eyes, only a blurred, distorted image, spiritual healing has proved the lens through which we have caught at last a clear, unclouded vision of the Christ. The irrevocable conviction, the certain knowledge that He lives is the miracle which transcends all others.

Appendix

A. The Healing Miracles of Jesus

Two blind men: Matt. 9:27–31
The dumb demoniac: Matt. 9:32–33
Deaf and dumb man: Mark 7:31–37
Blind man at Bethsaida: Mark 8:22–26
Widow of Nain's son: Luke 7:11–17
Ten lepers: Luke 17:11–19
Woman whom Satan had bound: Luke 13:11–17
Man with dropsy: Luke 14:1–6
Ear of Malchus: Luke 22:50–51
The Nobleman's son: John 4:46–54
Impotent man at Bethesda: John 5:1–21
Man born blind: John 9:1–7
Lazarus: John 11:32–44
The Syrophenician's daughter: Mark 7:24–30. Matt. 15:21–28
The centurion's servant: Matt. 8:5–13. Luke 7:1–10
The blind and dumb demoniac: Matt. 12:22. Luke 11:14
The "possessed" man in synagogue: Mark 1:21–28. Luke 4:33–37
Peter's mother-in-law: Matt. 8:14–15. Mark 1:29–31. Luke 4:38–39
Two demoniacs: Matt. 8:28–34. Mark 5:2–20. Luke 8:27–39
The leper: Matt. 8:1–4. Mark 1:40–45. Luke 5:12–14
Daughter of Jairus: Matt. 9:18–26. Mark 5:21–43. Luke 8:40–56
Woman with an issue of blood: Matt. 9:20–22. Mark 5:25–43. Luke
    8:43–48

A paralytic: Matt. 9:1–8. Mark 2:1–12. Luke 5:18–26
Man's withered hand: Matt. 12:9–13. Mark 3:1–5. Luke 6:6–10
Lunatic (epileptic) boy: Matt. 17:14–21. Mark 9:14–29. Luke 9: 37–43
Blind men: Matt. 20:29–34. Mark 10:46–52. Luke 18:35–43

B. THE MULTITUDES HEALED BY JESUS

St. Matthew 4:23–24	St. Mark 1:32–34, 39
8:16–17	3:7–11
9:35–36	6:5, 53–56
11:4–5	St. Luke 4:40–41
12:15	5:15
14:14, 34–36	6:17–19
15:30–31	7:21–22
19:1–2	9:11
21:14	13:32
	St. John 6:2

Some Books for Further Reading

Banks, John G., *Manual of Christian Healing*. San Diego, California: St. Luke's Press, 1953.

Beard, Rebecca, *Everyman's Search; Everyman's Goal; Everyman's Adventure*. Wells, Vermont: Merrybrook Press, 1950.

Carrel, Alexis, *The Voyage to Lourdes*. New York: Harper & Brothers, 1950.

Cliffe, A. E., *Let Go and Let God*. New York: Prentice-Hall, Inc., 1951.

Conkling, Wallace E., *Health and Salvation*. New York: Morehouse-Gorham, 1952.

Cranston, Ruth, *The Miracle of Lourdes*. New York: McGraw-Hill, 1955.

Dawson, George Gordon, *Healing: Pagan and Christian*. London: S.P.C.K., 1935.

Frost, Evelyn, *Christian Healing*. London: A. R. Mowbray, 1940.

Gross, Don, *The Case for Spiritual Healing*. New York: Thomas Nelson & Sons, 1958.

Hutchison, Harry, *Highway to Healing*. Evesham, England: Arthur James, Ltd., 1956.

Iklin, A. Graham, *New Concepts of Healing*. London: Hodder and Stroughton, 1955.

Jones, C. D., *Spiritual Healing*. New York: Longmans, Green & Co., 1955.

Jones, E. Stanley, *Abundant Living*. London: Abingdon Press, 1942.

Kew, Clifton E. and Clinton J., *You Can Be Healed.* New York: Prentice-Hall, Inc., 1953.

Neal, Emily Gardiner, *A Reporter Finds God Through Spiritual Healing.* New York: Morehouse-Gorham, 1956.

Oursler, Will, *The Healing Power of Faith.* New York: Hawthorne Books, Inc., 1957.

Portsmouth, William, *Healing Prayer.* Evesham, England: Arthur James, Ltd., 1954.

Salmon, Elsie, *He Heals Today.* Evesham, England: Arthur James, Ltd., 1951.

Sanford, Agnes, *The Healing Light.* St. Paul, Minnesota: Macalester Park Publishing Company, 1947.

Scherzer, Carl J., *The Church and Healing.* Philadelphia: Westminster Press, 1950.

Tournier, Paul, *A Doctor's Casebook in the Light of the Bible.* London: Camelot Press, Ltd., 1954.

Weatherhead, Leslie D., *Psychology, Religion and Health.* New York: Abingdon-Cokesbury, 1951.

Woodard, Christopher, *A Doctor Heals by Faith.* London: Max Parrish Co., Ltd., 1953.

Pamphlets

Dwyer, Walter, *Spiritual Healing in the U.S. and Great Britain.* New York: Samuel Weiser, Inc., n.d.

Eggleston, Louise, *Answered Prayer.* Norfolk, Virginia: World Literacy Prayer Group, Ghent Methodist Church, n.d.

Murray, J. A. C., *Fundamentals of the Ministry of Healing.* London: Guild of Health, n.d.

Price, Alfred, *Healing—The Gift of God; Religion and Health; Spiritual Aids for Healing the Sick.* Philadelphia: St. Stephen's Episcopal Church, n.d.

Tracts

Tracts by Ethel T. and John G. Banks. St. Luke's Press, 2243 Front Street, San Diego, California. This press has, or will procure, most of the aforementioned books.

SHARING. An International Journal of Christian Healing. Published monthly. Editor: Ethel T. Banks, 2243 Front Street, San Diego, California.